The Flavor of Asia

The Flavor of Asia

Reynaldo Alejandro

Beaufort Books, Inc.

New York / Toronto

This book was conceived and produced by The Photographic Book Company, Inc., for Beaufort Books, Inc.

Library of Congress Cataloging in Publication Data

Alejandro, Reynaldo G.
The Flavor of Asia.
Includes index.
1. Cookery, Oriental. I. Title.
TX724.5.A1A45 1984 641.595 84-11117
ISBN 0-8253-0244-7

Published in the United States by Beaufort Books, Inc., New York.
Published simultaneously in Canada by General Publishing Co. Limited

Printed in Hong Kong

10 9 8 7 6 5 4 3 2 1

To my aunts Presentacion, Victoria, and Virginia
and to
Marie, Mercedes, and Lee
who made me see the wonders of the East and West

Acknowledgments

In the making of this book, I am indebted for the help, support, and assistance of Minnie Bernardino, Bruna P. Sril, John Lowy, Marie Dizon, Madie Guevara, the Philippine Ministry of Tourism (New York), Linda Castillo, Richard Liu, Tran-Q-Thenth, Le-X-Thang, Patrick Wang, Jojo Banaag, Ellen Lochaya, and Eli Lovina; to Don Schrader and my editor, Linda Weinraub; and most especially to Herb Taylor and Cora Sibal, whose foresight and dedication made this book possible. I am also grateful to all those cooks and food writers who have paved the trail in popularizing and documenting the cuisines of Asia.

Contents

Introduction

Food historians say that cooking was born in Asia, in the area known today as China. It may have started when Peking Man discovered he could use fire to warm his body and thaw his food in the cold season. It was probably from this thawing technique that cooking was born.

Today, Asia constitutes the world's most populous region. It has contributed to the development of good taste and gastronomic adventure throughout the world, and has influenced many lifestyles and cultures. To consider the cuisines of Asia, one must survey and understand the huge family tree of cookery that emerged from this cradle of human civilization.

Chinese cuisine is the cornerstone of the cuisines of other Asians. It has influenced widely and deeply the cooking of Indonesia, Burma, Malaysia, Singapore, Mongolia, the Philippines, Japan, and Korea. In fact, the whole of Asia and much of the rest of the world have been touched by the influence of Chinese cuisine. Other—more specifically, European—influences on Asian cuisine have occurred more locally and, of course, more recently. The colonization of Indonesia by the Dutch, Vietnam by the French, and the Philippines by the Spanish (and, since the early twentieth century, the American presence), have all contributed European tastes, ingredients, and methods of cooking to Oriental cuisine—a gift that has been returned a thousandfold.

Asia, the largest and most populous of the continents, has an extensively varied geography. From seacoast to high mountains, water is abundant, and the products of the ocean, lakes, rivers, and streams comprise a large proportion of the Asian diet. Rice is, of course, the staple crop, and with vegetables and fish dominates the Asian cuisine. Beef, and to a greater extent pork and poultry, also contribute to the protein base of Asian meals, and legumes and cereals are consumed as well. In addition to these are the more exotic (to the Westerner) specialties—sharks' fins, birds' nests, sea urchins, various seaweeds, to name the better known. To the oriental cook, most of these ingredients are less bizarre than merely rare (and therefore expensive) delicacies which, rather like caviar, are consumed on special occasions by those who can afford them. Whether his ingredients are rare or common, the Asian cook, by his creativity, is always the master of his environment.

More than the ingredients, it is the skill and ingenuity of the Asian cooks that produce the exquisite and wonderfully varied cuisines of Asia. The cooks of Asia look upon cooking as an art rather than a skill, and as a means of intensely personal expression. One seldom sees a true Asian cook using a cookbook; almost every cooking principle is borne in the mind. Open-fire stoves are the center of the Asian kitchen, and the method of cooking atop a fire is the most common. Steaming, parboiling, boiling, frying, and grilling are the most popular techniques. Cooking is traditionally done from scratch, and the cooks, chefs, and gourmets of the region have a deep tradition of innovation, creativity, and imagination.

Asians love to combine the *yin* and *yang* of tastes, juxtaposing sweet and sour, salty and sour, salty and bitter. But in this mixture of tastes is a unifying element—the use of spices and herbs is always designed to bring out the best of tastes from the combined ingredients. Fish dishes almost always contain ginger as a spice; garlic is combined with meat and poultry; herbs, curry, and pepper accompany vegetables.

Because so much of Asia is tropical (only northern China, Japan, and Korea truly experience the four seasons), Asians have developed a variety of methods intended to preserve foods and prolong the life of prepared dishes. Pickling, drying, smoking, and roasting are a few of the techniques used for the preservation of food.

True Asian cooks approach food with a measure of reverence. Rice is a staple food that has passed from one rite to another as a "gift of the gods." Coconut, another basic ingredient and a true companion of rice dishes, is also revered as the "tree of life" for its versatility and sustenance-giving qualities. Cooking and eating are twin delights of Asian culinary culture, and in the region's tradition of hospitality, food reigns supreme as an instrument of goodwill, unity, and peace.

Asian cuisine is varied and homogeneous at the same time. It may be simple or complex to prepare, the ingredients exotic and costly or common and inexpensive. Whatever its ingredients and methods of preparation, Asian cooking is always adaptable to any environment, aesthetic in presentation, sensual to a supreme degree, and considerate of any human condition. Each ingredient, each method of preparation, is designed to balance another, either by contrast or complement, in terms of both taste and texture. Different ingredients in each dish, and different dishes in each meal, are always selected to reinforce the inherent nature of the ingredients, a philosophy which constantly inspires the creativity of the individual cook.

It is obviously impossible to catalog all the wonderful recipes of Asia, all the marvels of the region's various national cuisines, all the delights of the Asian table. However, in selecting the recipes of the nations included in this book, I was guided by the thought of providing an overview through which the reader might glimpse the incredibly ancient history of Asian cooking. Chapters are therefore spiced with bits and pieces of historical notes, but these are kept brief so as not to distract from the recipes of the region. The chapters are arranged according to courses instead of regions, in deference to the Western cook's accustomed approach to the planning of a meal; however, within each chapter, dishes of each nation are grouped together.

The rewards of learning Asian cookery are great. They expand the cook's understanding of those culinary traditions which, as much as traditions of art, politics, or language, shape and move a people's culture. To understand Asian cuisine is to appreciate the harmony, philosophy, humanity, and world outlook of the Asians. This outlook may be best summed up by a tale in the old Burmese chronicles about a king partaking of food: each meal must always consist of "three hundred dishes, salted and spiced, sweet and sharp, bitter and hot, luscious and parching."

—Reynaldo Alejandro
Greenwich Village, New York City

Appetizers

The appetizers of Asia make excellent and tasty beginnings for any meal. They can be enjoyed with chilled beer or with piping hot and fragrant tea, with wines, mixed drinks, and fruit punches.

These finger-foods are piquant, aromatic, spicy, and always full of surprises. They come in various shapes—small crescents of seafood, meatballs dusted with spices, pork- and chicken-skin cracklings, strips of crisp vegetables, or rolls of paper-thin flour wrappers filled with ground meat and minced vegetables. Sometimes they are bite-sized pieces of skewered meat, fruit, or vegetables, grilled or turned over barbecue fires. Tidbits of fish, meat, and poultry—tails, wings, spareribs, liver—are seasoned to perfection, deep-fried, and served with sauces blending the flavors of sweet and sour.

Almost always, these little dishes are presented as miniature food sculptures, garnished with carved slices of fresh vegetables or with pickled greens. They exude an appeal that captivates the senses of taste, sight, and smell.

The selection of recipes in this chapter is designed to bring out the best in your drinks, complement the mellow flavor of your Asian beer, and whet your appetite for a meal to enjoy and remember.

Ling Mun Gai

CHINA

(Chicken Liver)

- 8 ounces chicken livers, cut in half
- ¼ cup lemon juice
- ½ cup soy sauce
- ½ cup flour
- ¾ cup onion, finely minced
- 3 tablespoons vegetable oil

1. Marinate halved chicken livers in lemon juice and soy sauce in refrigerator overnight.
2. Drain and dredge in flour.
3. Heat oil in frying pan and fry livers and onion until brown.
4. Serve immediately.

SERVES 4

Hamaguri-Zuke

JAPAN

(Pickled Clams)

- 3 cups littleneck clams, shelled
- 4 tablespoons cider vinegar
- 4 tablespoons soy sauce
- ½ cup sake
- 4 tablespoons sugar

1. Marinate all ingredients overnight in refrigerator.
2. Drain and serve.

SERVES 4

Frikadel Djagoeng

INDONESIA

(Corn Fritters)

- ¾ cup water
- 1 egg, beaten
- 1 cup rice flour
- ¼ teaspoon ground cumin
- ½ teaspoon ground coriander
- ½ teaspoon ground black pepper
- 1 teaspoon salt
- 2 cups fresh or thawed frozen corn kernels
- ½ cup scallions, finely minced
- 2 cups vegetable oil

1. Blend water, egg, and flour to make a smooth paste.
2. Add cumin, coriander, pepper, and salt, and mix thoroughly until smooth. Add corn kernels and scallions.
3. Heat oil in a deep frying pan. Drop in 3–4 balls of batter, each about 1 tablespoonful, at a time. Fry until brown.
4. Drain on paper towel before serving.

SERVES 4

Rodi Lapis Sambal

MALAYSIA

(Malaysian Sandwich)

8 ounces dried shrimp

Water

2 fresh red chilies, seeded and thinly sliced

4 tablespoons vegetable oil

3 cups onion, finely minced

4 slices fresh white bread, cut into bite-size pieces

1. Soak dried shrimp in water 15 minutes. Drain.
2. In food processor, process chilies and shrimp to a paste-like consistency.
3. In frying pan, heat oil and sauté onion until transparent. Add shrimp and chili mixture. Stir well. Remove and cool.
4. Spread onto half the white bread slices and top with remaining slices.

SERVES 4

Panaeng Neua

THAILAND

(Beef Balls in Peanut Sauce)

2 tablespoons vegetable oil

2 tablespoons garlic, finely minced

1 pound lean ground beef, shaped into balls (about marble size)

½ cup all-purpose flour

2 tablespoons red curry paste (*krung gaeng ped*)

1 cup coconut milk

2 tablespoons peanuts, ground

2 tablespoons sugar

2 tablespoons fish sauce

2 teaspoons fresh mint, chopped

1. In large saucepan, heat oil, and fry garlic for 1 minute. Remove garlic.
2. Roll beef balls in flour, and fry until brown. Remove and drain on paper towels. Set aside.
3. Fry red curry paste 3 minutes, mixing thoroughly. Add coconut milk and ground peanuts. Blend well to a smooth consistency.
4. Stir in sugar and fish sauce. Drop in beef balls. Simmer over low heat 10 minutes.
5. Transfer to a serving dish while hot, and garnish with fresh mint.

SERVES 4

Ma Uon

THAILAND

(Fat Horses)

- 2 chicken breasts, boned, skinned, and chopped
- 1 cup cooked shredded crabmeat
- 1 cup ground pork
- 2 tablespoons coriander root, finely minced
- 1½ teaspoons freshly ground black pepper
- 2 tablespoons garlic, finely minced
- 2 tablespoons fish sauce
- 4 tablespoons coconut milk
- 2 tablespoons sugar
- 3 eggs, beaten
- ½ cup scallions, finely minced
- coriander leaves
- banana leaves or small paper cups

1. In food processor, puree chicken breast, crabmeat, and pork until smooth.
2. Add coriander root, black pepper, garlic, fish sauce, coconut milk, sugar, and eggs.
3. Transfer to individual cups or banana leaves, and top with scallions.
4. Place on a steaming rack over boiling water, on top of the stove, and steam until mixture is firm. Let cool.
5. Invert cups onto a large serving platter, and garnish with coriander leaves.

SERVES 4–6

Kai Kem

THAILAND

(Salted Eggs)

- 12 cups water
- 1 cup salt
- 10 large eggs, uncooked

1. Boil water and salt. Set aside and cool.
2. Put uncooked eggs in large crock or glass jar with lid and cover with cooled salt water.
3. Cover crock or glass jar with lid. Put in a cool, dry place for one month.
4. When ready to use, remove eggs and hardboil them. Serve sliced as an appetizer.

SERVES 10

Gai Yik

CHINA

(Chicken Wings)

- 2 dozen chicken wings
- 2 cups soy sauce
- 2 teaspoons prepared mustard
- 2 teaspoons ginger root, freshly grated
- ½ cup sugar
- 2 teaspoons garlic, finely grated

1. Marinate chicken wings, soy sauce, mustard, ginger, sugar, and garlic in refrigerator overnight.
2. Drain, and bake 1 hour at 350°F.
3. Place under broiler for 3 minutes. Serve hot.

SERVES 4

Wonton

CHINA

(Fried Dumplings)

- ½ pound ground pork
- 2 tablespoons scallions, finely minced
- ½ cup fresh mushrooms, finely minced
- ¼ teaspoon salt
- ⅛ teaspoon black pepper, freshly ground
- 1 egg, beaten
- wonton wrappers (available fresh or frozen in Oriental groceries)
- 2–3 cups vegetable oil
- Chinese mustard

1. In a mixing bowl, combine pork, scallions, mushrooms, salt, pepper, and egg. Mix thoroughly.
2. Place half a teaspoonful of mixture in center of each wonton wrapper. Fold over one point to the other to make a triangle and bring the two ends together. Moisten with water so the ends stick together.
3. Heat oil in a frying pan and fry the wonton. Drain on paper towel.
4. Serve hot with Chinese mustard as a sauce.

SERVES 6

Beya Kyaw

BURMA

(Split Pea Fritters)

1 cup split peas

2 medium onions, finely minced

2 fresh red chilies, finely minced

½ teaspoon ground turmeric

½ teaspoon salt

oil for deep-frying

1 onion, sliced

2 lemon wedges

1. Soak the peas overnight in water. Drain. Place in food processor and grind to a paste-like consistency.
2. Mix the onions, chilies, turmeric, and salt with the pea paste.
3. Heat oil in deep fryer.
4. Shape mixture into patties ½-inch thick and deep-fry until golden brown. Drain and arrange on a platter with lemon wedges and onion slices as garnish.

SERVES 4

Kim Tien Ke

VIETNAM

(Golden Coins)

- 2 whole chicken breasts, skinned, boned, and cut into 1-inch squares
- 4 pieces Chinese sausage, sliced ¼-inch thick
- 1 pound boiled ham, cubed
- 1½ teaspoons sugar
- 1 teaspoon Five Spice powder
- 5 tablespoons soy sauce
- 1 teaspoon ground black pepper
- 2 tablespoons oyster sauce
- ½ cup dry white wine

1. Mix all of the above ingredients together and marinate overnight.
2. On a skewer, alternate the chicken, sausages, and ham. Grill over charcoal until they become a golden brown color.
3. Serve hot.

SERVES 8–10

Ukoy

THE PHILIPPINES

(Bean Sprout Fritters)

Batter:

2 eggs

1 cup cornstarch

1 tablespoon *achuete* juice

Filling:

1 pound bean sprouts

12 medium-size shrimps, with shell

1 piece bean curd, cut into thin pieces

¼ pound ground pork

fat for frying (enough to cover fritters)

½ teaspoon shrimp paste

white vinegar, salt, and crushed garlic to taste

1. Beat eggs very well; add cornstarch and *achuete* juice.
2. In a saucer, place 2 tablespoons of batter; arrange some bean sprouts, shrimp, bean curd, ground pork, and ½ teaspoon of shrimp paste on top.
3. Cover with 2 tablespoons of batter and deep-fat fry.
4. Serve hot with white vinegar, salt, and crushed garlic.

YIELD: 12 FRITTERS

Empanaditas

THE PHILIPPINES

(Meat-Filled Turnovers)

Pastry:

1 14-ounce package of double-crust pastry (makes about 12–16 four-inch squares).

Filling:

1 tablespoon vegetable or corn oil

2 tablespoons garlic, minced

¼ cup onion, minced

¼ cup tomatoes, minced

1 cup ground veal

1 cup ground pork

1 cup ground or chopped chicken

salt

pepper

1 cup chopped hardboiled eggs (4 or 5 eggs)

1 cup sweet pickles, chopped

1. Flatten pastry to a thickness of ⅛ inch. Cut into 4-inch squares. Set aside.
2. In medium skillet, heat oil. Sauté garlic, onion, and tomatoes. Cook until garlic is brown and onions turn transparent.
3. Add veal, pork, and chicken. Season with salt and pepper. Cook 20–25 minutes, until meat is done.
4. Add eggs and pickles. Cook 5 minutes longer.
5. Allow mixture to cool.
6. Preheat oven to 400°F. Fill each piece of dough with a teaspoonful of the mixture. Fold to form a triangle. Moisten edges with water and seal. Arrange on a cookie sheet and bake the pastries for 25–30 minutes.

SERVES 6–8

Lumpia Shanghai

THE PHILIPPINES

(Philippine Fried Egg Rolls, Shanghai Style)

½ pound pork, ground

½ pound shrimps, shelled and chopped fine

½ cup water chestnuts, chopped

½ cup green onions, chopped fine

1 egg

1 tablespoon soy sauce

1 teaspoon freshly ground pepper

1 teaspoon salt

1 package egg roll wrappers (sold in Oriental stores)

½ cup cooking oil

1. Combine pork, shrimp, water chestnuts, green onion, egg, and soy sauce.
2. Season with salt and pepper.
3. Place a level tablespoon of filling on each egg roll wrapper, fold, and seal with a few drops of water.
4. Deep-fry in hot oil and drain on paper towel.
5. Serve with sweet-and-sour sauce.

SERVES 6–8

Soups

An Asian meal is not complete without a tureen of soup served with the rest of the dishes. However, unlike Western custom, soup does not generally open the meal; instead, it is brought to the table in the company of a meat or fish entree, with a rice dish and condiments.

Almost all Asian meals—breakfast, lunch, and dinner—feature some kind of soup. At times, soup is the sole dish of a meal; it may also be taken as a filling snack at mid-morning or mid-afternoon, rather like the British tea or bouillon.

The Chinese, Koreans, and Japanese are masters in the making of light, velvety, savory soups that feature a variety of ingredients from land and sea. In the Philippines, Thailand, and other Southeast Asian countries, soups are spiked with a souring fruit or plant. Indonesian *sotos*, which are served to moisten rice, are broth-based dishes featuring seafood, cubes of meat, fine threads of noodle, bean paste, or julienned vegetables. The Vietnamese make soups with rich broths, textured with the meat of chicken and pork and bite-size slices of vegetables, and flavored with mint leaves. In Korea, the favorite soup is *yukkai jang kuku*, a one-pot dish consisting of thin slices of beef and young spring onions in a hot stock of chilies, seasoned with garlic and ground sesame seeds.

In all events, the secret of a good Asian soup is a rich stock and a skillful blending of fresh and preserved ingredients. The recipes in this selection of soups are intended to give you a tour of the special and everyday broth-based dishes of the region.

The soups of Asia represent a variety of gestures during the course of a meal—sipped at intervals, poured in modest spoonfuls over the staple rice, or downed for a refreshing punctuation to a varied course of delicacies. Served in individual bowls or in communal tureens, they can be the mainstays of Asian menus throughout the four seasons.

Chapyung Ti Hinyu

BURMA

(Pumpkin or Squash Soup)

- 6 cups beef broth
- 1 medium onion, finely minced
- 1½ teaspoons anchovy paste
- 2 cloves garlic, finely minced
- 1½ cups raw shrimp, shelled, deveined, and minced
- ¼ teaspoon ground dried chili peppers
- 5 cups pumpkin or winter squash, quartered and peeled

1. Bring beef broth to a boil. Add onion, anchovy paste, garlic, and shrimp and continue to boil in saucepan 5 minutes.
2. Add chili peppers and pumpkin or squash and continue to boil 5 minutes more.
3. Reduce heat, and simmer until pumpkin or squash is tender or soft, about 10 minutes.
4. Serve hot.

SERVES 4

Hin Thee Hin Ywet

BURMA

(Green Vegetable Soup)

4 cups water

1 medium onion, chopped

2 cloves garlic, crushed

2 tablespoons pounded dried shrimp

½ teaspoon shrimp paste

½ teaspoon salt

1½ teaspoons soy sauce

½ pound spinach, watercress, or mustard greens

1. Bring water to a boil in a saucepan. Add onion and garlic. Boil 10 minutes.
2. Add dried shrimp, shrimp paste, salt, and soy sauce. Reduce heat.
3. Stir in green vegetables and continue simmering 3 minutes.
4. Serve hot.

SERVES 4

Canh Chua

VIETNAM

(Sour Fish Soup)

1 pound red snapper (sea bass or grouper may be used)

1 onion, quartered

1½ teaspoons fish sauce

1 tablespoon tamarind liquid (or 2 tablespoons lemon juice)

2 quarts water

3 tomatoes, quartered

2 stalks celery, cut julienne style

1½ cup bean sprouts

1 teaspoon ground pepper

1. In saucepan, cook fish, onion, and fish sauce 5 minutes, over low heat.
2. Add tamarind liquid and water and bring to boil. Cook 5 minutes.
3. Add tomatoes and celery, and continue boiling until tender.
4. Turn off heat, add bean sprouts and pepper. Mix well.
5. Serve hot.

SERVES 4–6

Soto Ayam

MALAYSIA

(Chicken Soup)

- 4 teaspoons salt
- 6 cups water
- 1 chicken, whole (2–3 pounds)
- 1 teaspoon whole black peppercorns
- 1 cup onion, chopped
- 3 tablespoons vegetable oil
- 1 cup onion, finely minced
- 6 curry leaves
- 1 teaspoon fresh ginger root, finely grated
- 2 teaspoon garlic, finely minced
- ½ teaspoon dried shrimp paste
- 2 teaspoons ground coriander
- ½ teaspoon ground turmeric
- ½ teaspoon ground cumin
- 3 finely grated candlenuts (*buah keras*)
- 1 ounce rice vermicelli, soaked in water, drained, and cut in 6-inch lengths
- 3 potatoes, peeled, cooked, and diced
- 1 tablespoon lemon juice
- 2 hardboiled eggs, finely chopped
- 1 cup scallions, finely chopped

1. Boil chicken in large pot with water, salt, peppercorns, and chopped onions. Let cool. Strain stock into bowl and set aside.
2. Debone and remove skin of chicken and cut meat in strips. Set aside.
3. In a large saucepan, heat oil and fry minced onion and curry leaves until onions turns transparent. Add ginger, garlic, shrimp paste. Continue stirring and simmer 5 minutes. Add coriander, turmeric, cumin, and candlenuts. Fry, continuing to stir, 2 minutes.
4. Add chicken stock and boil 5 minutes. Simmer over low heat another 5 minutes. Add rice vermicelli and continue cooking 5 more minutes.
5. Add chicken meat, potatoes, and lemon juice. Serve hot and garnish with eggs and scallions.

SERVES 6

Gay Lim Sook Mi Gai Tong

CHINA

(Chicken and Sweet Corn Soup)

- 2 chicken breasts, finely chopped
- 1 egg white
- ½ teaspoon salt
- ¼ teaspoon pepper
- 4 cups chicken stock
- 1 8-ounce can sweet corn
- 3 tablespoons soy sauce
- ⅓ cup Chinese wine
- 1 teaspoon sesame oil
- 2 teaspoons cornstarch
- 2 tablespoons water
- ⅓ cup shredded cooked ham

1. Combine egg white, salt, and pepper and pour over chicken. Marinate 1 hour.
2. In large saucepan, boil chicken stock. Add corn, soy sauce, Chinese wine, and sesame oil. Simmer 5 minutes.
3. Add chicken and marinade, and continue simmering 10 minutes more.
4. Mix cornstarch and water, and stir into soup. Simmer another 5 minutes.
5. Serve hot with shredded ham on top.

SERVES 4

Ca Nau Ca Chua

VIETNAM

(Tomato Fish Soup)

1 pound cod (or snapper, or bass), cut in serving pieces

2 tablespoons vegetable oil

3 tomatoes, quartered

1 onion, quartered

2 tablespoons fish sauce

2 quarts water

2 celery stalks, cut julienne style

2 tablespoons fresh dill, minced

1 teaspoon ground black pepper

1. In large saucepan, brown fish lightly in oil.
2. Add tomatoes, onion, and fish sauce, and simmer 4 minutes.
3. Add water, and bring to boil until tomatoes are soft (about 15 minutes).
4. Add celery and dill and season with pepper and additional fish sauce.
5. Serve hot.

SERVES 4–6

Dom Yam Gung

THAILAND

(Hot and Sour Shrimp Soup)

- 2 pounds shrimp, shelled and deveined (save the shells)
- 1 tablespoon vegetable oil
- 2 green fresh chilies, minced
- 6 citrus leaves
- 1 teaspoon lime zest, minced
- 8 cups chicken stock
- 2 teaspoons salt
- 1 cup lemon grass, cut in 1-inch lengths
- ½ cup lime juice
- 1 tablespoon fish sauce
- ½ cup scallions, chopped
- 1 red fresh chili, minced
- 2 tablespoons coriander leaves, chopped

1. In large saucepan, fry shrimp shells in oil 5 minutes.
2. Add green chilies, citrus leaves, lime zest, chicken stock, salt, and lemon grass. Simmer 30 minutes over moderate heat.
3. Strain the liquid and return it to saucepan. Bring to a boil.
4. Add lime juice, fish sauce, and shrimps. Cook for 4 minutes.
5. Transfer to a soup tureen and garnish with scallions, red chili, and coriander leaves.
6. Serve hot.

SERVES 6

Kao Dom

THAILAND

(Rice Soup)

5 cups chicken stock

1 cup ground pork

1 cup cooked rice

2 tablespoons fish sauce

5 eggs

1 tablespoon fresh ginger root, finely minced

1 tablespoon coriander leaves, chopped

½ cup scallions, minced

1. In large saucepan, bring chicken stock to a boil. Add ground pork. Continue boiling and separate pork pieces.
2. Add cooked rice and fish sauce. Continue to simmer over moderate heat for 10 minutes.
3. Break eggs into 5 separate soup bowls. Pour some soup into each.
4. Garnish with fresh ginger root, coriander, and scallions.
5. Serve hot.

SERVES 5

Gorigomtang

KOREA

(Oxtail Soup)

1 oxtail, cut in 10 pieces

8 cups water

1 teaspoon salt

3 slices fresh ginger

Sauce:

½ cup scallions, finely minced

¼ teaspoon ground black pepper

1 tablespoon sesame oil

4 tablespoons soy sauce

1 teaspoon fresh ginger, finely minced

1½ tablespoons garlic, finely minced

1 tablespoon toasted, crushed sesame seeds

1. In a large saucepan, bring the oxtail, water, salt, and ginger to a boil. Simmer until tender, about 2 hours. Skim off any froth that may appear on the surface.
2. Remove oxtail from broth, cut into bite-size pieces, and return to the pan.
3. Combine sauce ingredients in a separate bowl. Mix well.
4. Serve the sauce as a dipping sauce for pieces of oxtail.
5. Serve soup hot.

SERVES 4

Suan La Tang

CHINA

(Hot and Sour Soup, Peking Style)

- 4 ounces pork tenderloin, shredded
- ⅛ teaspoon salt
- ⅛ teaspoon freshly ground pepper
- 7 teaspoons cornstarch
- 4 cups chicken stock
- ½ cup dried Chinese mushrooms, soaked in warm water, then shredded
- ½ cup carrot, parboiled and shredded
- ½ cup canned bamboo shoots, shredded
- ½ cup cooked ham, shredded
- 1 teaspoon salt
- ½ cup scallions, finely minced
- ½ teaspoon freshly ground pepper
- 2 tablespoons soy sauce
- 4 tablespoons water
- 2 tablespoons vinegar
- 2 tablespoons sesame oil
- 3 eggs, beaten

1. Sprinkle pork with salt, pepper, and 1 teaspoon cornstarch. Set aside.
2. In stockpot, bring chicken stock to a boil, and add mushrooms, carrot, bamboo shoots, and ham. Cook 5 minutes.
3. Add salt, scallions, pepper, soy sauce, 6 teaspoons cornstarch mixed with 4 tablespoons water, vinegar, and sesame oil. Stir constantly until soup thickens.
4. Slowly pour in beaten eggs while stirring gently.
5. Serve hot.

SERVES 4

Dahn Far Tong

CHINA

(Egg Flower Soup)

- 5 cups chicken stock
- 1 teaspoon sesame oil
- 2 tablespoons Chinese wine
- ¼ teaspoon salt
- 4 eggs, beaten
- salt to taste
- ½ cup scallions, finely chopped

1. In large pot, bring chicken stock to a boil. Add sesame oil and Chinese wine.
2. Combine salt and eggs, and pour slowly into boiling soup, stirring slowly.
3. Adjust salt seasoning to taste. Garnish with scallions and serve immediately.

SERVES 4

Gup Guy T'ang

CHINA

(Clam Soup)

- 3 cups clam juice
- 3 cups chicken broth
- ¾ cup onion, finely minced
- 3 cups clams, minced
- 3 tablespoons soy sauce
- 3 tablespoons fresh parsley, minced
- 2 tablespoons dry sherry

1. In large saucepan, mix clam juice and chicken broth. Bring to a boil. Add onions and clams. Simmer over moderate heat 15 minutes.
2. Add soy sauce, parsley, and dry sherry. Continue to simmer another 5 minutes. Serve hot.

SERVES 6

Bam-I Nahm

THAILAND

(Egg Noodle Soup)

8 ounces fresh egg noodles

1 cup beef, chicken, or seafood, cooked and chopped

2 tablespoons fresh coriander, minced

2 tablespoons scallions, minced

2 tablespoons celery leaves, minced

1 teaspoon sesame oil

4 cups chicken stock

fish sauce to taste

1. Boil water in large stock pot. Add egg noodles. When water boils again, add more cold water and bring to boil a third time. Drain and set aside.
2. In 4 large soup bowls, arrange noodles at bottom and put the cooked meat, coriander, scallions, celery leaves, and sesame oil on top of noodles.
3. Boil chicken stock and pour gently into soup bowls.
4. Season with fish sauce.
5. Serve hot.

SERVES 4

Gogi Kuk

KOREA

(Beef and Vegetable Soup)

- 3 tablespoons vegetable oil
- 8 ounces round or chuck steak, cut in 1-inch cubes
- ½ cup scallions, finely minced
- 2 teaspoons garlic, finely minced
- 6 dried Chinese mushrooms, soaked and sliced (discard stems)
- 1 teaspoon hot bean sauce
- 8 cups beef stock
- 2 tablespoons soy sauce
- 1 teaspoon salt
- 1 tablespoon sherry
- ½ teaspoon ground black pepper
- 2 teaspoons sesame oil

1. Heat oil in large saucepan. Add steak and sauté until brown.
2. Add scallions, garlic, and mushrooms, and stir-fry 2 minutes.
3. Add bean sauce, beef stock, soy sauce, salt, sherry, and black pepper. Bring to a boil, then reduce heat and simmer 15 minutes.
4. Add sesame oil and serve hot.

SERVES 6

Sayur Lodeh

INDONESIA

(Eggplant and Prawn Soup)

2 tablespoons peanut oil

3 cloves garlic, finely minced

1 cup onion, finely minced

1 fresh red chili, seeded and chopped

1 cup ripe tomatoes, cubed

2 curry leaves

3 cups chicken stock

3 cups eggplant, peeled and diced

1 teaspoon brown sugar

1 cup coconut milk

½ teaspoon salt

5 ounces fresh prawns (or shrimps), shelled, deveined, and cut in small pieces

1. In large saucepan, sauté oil, garlic, onion, and chili until onion is transparent. Add tomatoes and curry leaves, and simmer for 8 minutes. Add chicken stock. Simmer 15 minutes more.
2. Add eggplant and cook 10 minutes until eggplant is tender. Add sugar, coconut milk, and salt. Simmer 5 minutes more and add prawns. Remove from heat (prawns will be cooked by the heat of the other ingredients).
3. Pour in soup bowls. Serve hot.

SERVES 4

Soto Ajam

INDONESIA

(Chicken Soup)

- 1 chicken, whole (2–3 pounds)
- 10 cups water
- 1 tablespoon salt
- 1 cup scallions, minced
- 2 curry leaves
- 3 tablespoons vegetable oil
- 2 gloves garlic, crushed
- ½ cup onion, finely minced
- 1 ¼-inch slice ginger
- ⅜ teaspoon ground coriander seeds
- ⅓ teaspoon turmeric
- ½ lemon

Garnishes:

- 4 boiled potatoes, peeled and sliced
- 1 cup soaked vermicelli noodles
- 3 tablespoons fried onion flakes
- ½ cup celery leaves, chopped
- 4 hard-boiled eggs, peeled and sliced
- ¾ cup scallions, finely minced

1. In large saucepan, boil chicken in 10 cups of water. Add salt, scallions, and curry leaves. Cook until tender. Set stock aside and drain chicken.
2. In another saucepan, sauté oil, garlic, onion, and ginger until transparent. Transfer to chicken stock together with coriander seeds and turmeric. Simmer 45 minutes.
3. Separate meat from chicken bones, and cut meat in thin strips. Discard skin and bones.
4. Mix chicken strips with garnishes in a large soup tureen. Pour stock on top. Squeeze lemon juice on top, serve hot.

SERVES 4

Sajur Terung Atau Labu

INDONESIA

(Zucchini or Eggplant Soup)

- 1/8 teaspoon cumin seeds
- 1/4 teaspoon coriander seeds
- 4 macadamia nuts or almonds
- 1/5 teaspoon turmeric
- 1 1/2 teaspoons ground chili
- 3 tablespoons vegetable oil or peanut oil
- 1 cup onion, finely minced
- 2 cloves garlic, chopped
- 1 1/2-inch slice ginger
- 4 tablespoons chicken or beef, chopped
- salt to taste
- 4 cups water
- 1/4 teaspoon *laos* powder
- 2 cups coconut milk
- 2 medium-size zucchini, (or eggplants or cucumbers), cut in 2-inch cubes
- 1 teaspoon lemon juice

1. In food processor, blend cumin seeds, coriander seeds, nuts, turmeric, and chili. Set aside.
2. Heat oil in saucepan, and sauté onion and garlic until transparent. Add ginger, meat, salt, and water, and bring to boil for 10 minutes.
3. Add processed ingredients and *laos* powder, and simmer about 20 minutes. Add coconut milk. Continue simmering another 15 minutes. Add vegetables, and continue simmering until vegetables are cooked.
4. Add lemon juice and serve hot.

SERVES 6

Sajur Kare

INDONESIA

(Curried Vegetable Soup)

- 3/8 teaspoon *laos* powder
- 1/2 teaspoon turmeric
- 2 cloves garlic, chopped
- 1 cup onion, finely minced
- 1 teaspoon vegetable oil
- 2 cups coconut milk
- 8 cups diced vegetables (cabbage, carrot, zucchini, potatoes, etc.)
- 1 stalk lemon grass, finely sliced
- 3 curry leaves

1. In food processor, puree *laos* powder, turmeric, garlic, onion, and oil to a smooth paste.
2. In a large saucepan, fry the paste 8 minutes, until cooked and aromatic. Add coconut milk. Bring mixture to a boil.
3. Add vegetables and simmer uncovered until tender (about 12 minutes).
4. Serve hot.

SERVES 4

Khao Poun

CAMBODIA

(Long Rice Soup)

1 cup soaked cellophane noodles, cut in 6-inch-long pieces

6 cups chicken stock

½ teaspoon salt

½ cup smoked ham, finely chopped

½ cup pork, finely minced

2 tablespoons water chestnuts, finely chopped

½ teaspoon cornstarch

3 teaspoons soy sauce

2 tablespoons scallions, finely minced

1. Boil chicken stock in large saucepan and drop in cellophane noodles. Add salt. Simmer over moderate heat 25 minutes.
2. Combine ham, pork, water chestnuts, cornstarch, and soy sauce. Mix well. Shape into small balls and drop into soup.
3. Boil another 15 minutes.
4. Serve hot, garnished with scallions.

SERVES 4

Samlor Chhrook

CAMBODIA and LAOS

(Pork Soup)

- 1 pound pork chops, meat separated from bones and chopped (use bones for stock)
- 1 tablespoon vegetable oil
- 3 tablespoons garlic, finely minced
- 1 tablespoon lemon juice
- 1 tablespoon fish sauce
- 2 teaspoons sugar
- 1 tablespoon fresh ginger root, finely minced
- 2 tablespoons fresh coriander leaves, chopped

1. Prepare stock, using pork bones and 8 cups water. Allow water to reduce to 6 cups.
2. In large saucepan, heat oil, and sauté garlic until light brown. Add chopped pork meat. Fry 3 minutes.
3. Add 6 cups of stock, lemon juice, fish sauce, sugar, and ginger. Simmer over moderate heat 40 minutes.
4. Serve hot, garnished with coriander leaves.

SERVES 4

Keng Som Kalampi

LAOS

(Sour Cabbage Soup)

- 1½ pounds pork butt, cut in serving pieces
- 4 cups water
- ¼ teaspoon salt
- ½ cup scallion bulbs
- 1 stalk lemon grass
- ½ tablespoon fish sauce
- ½ medium-size cabbage, cut in bite-size pieces
- 2 cups tomatoes, sliced
- ½ cup scallions, minced

1. Bring water to boil in large saucepan. Add pork butt, salt, scallion bulbs, lemon grass, and fish sauce. Simmer 10 minutes or until meat is done.
2. Add cabbage and tomatoes. Cook until cabbage is done (about 5 minutes).
3. Garnish with chopped scallions.
4. Serve hot.

SERVES 6

Keng Jeeg Kai

LAOS

(Shredded Chicken Soup)

- 1 whole chicken (2–3 pounds)
- 6 cups water
- 1 cup scallions, minced
- 1 teaspoon salt
- 1 cup onion, finely minced
- 1 cup peeled shallots
- ½ teaspoon fish sauce
- 2 heads garlic, peeled
- ½ teaspoon freshly ground black pepper
- ½ cup scallions, finely minced

1. In stockpot, boil chicken in 6 cups water with scallions and salt. When chicken is cooked, let cool, and strain broth. Set aside. Remove and discard skin and bones from chicken and shred meat. Set aside.
2. In same stockpot, pour in strained broth, and bring to boil.
3. Add minced onion, peeled shallots, fish sauce, and garlic. Simmer over moderate heat 30 minutes.
4. Add shredded chicken meat, pepper, and scallions.
5. Serve hot.

SERVES 6

Keng Bouad Mak Fak Kham

LAOS

(Pumpkin and Coconut Milk Soup)

- 6 cups pumpkin, peeled and cut in 1-inch cubes
- 2 8-ounce cans coconut milk
- 3 teaspoons shallots, finely minced
- 3 fresh coriander sprigs
- ⅛ teaspoon salt
- ½ teaspoon fish sauce
- ½ cup scallions, finely minced
- ⅛ teaspoon freshly ground black pepper

1. In large saucepan, combine pumpkin, coconut milk, shallots, and coriander sprigs. Bring to a boil.
2. Add salt and fish sauce. Let simmer until pumpkin is tender, about 10 minutes.
3. Garnish with minced scallions and pepper, and serve hot.

SERVES 4

Ise-Ebi To Kyuri No Soup

JAPAN

(Lobster-Cucumber Soup)

- 5 cups *dashi*
- 2 teaspoons sake
- 1 teaspoon soy sauce
- 2 cups lobster, cooked and cut up
- 8 dried mushrooms, soaked in water, stems removed, and drained
- 1 cucumber, thinly sliced
- 4 thin slices lemon rind

1. Boil *dashi*. Add sake and soy sauce. Add lobster, mushroom, and cucumber.
2. Immediately transfer into a serving tureen, and add lemon rind.
3. Serve immediately.

SERVES 4

Satsuma Jiru

JAPAN

(Vegetable and Noodle Miso)

¼ cup dried shrimp

3 cups water

1 cup turnip, shredded

½ cup onion, chopped

½ pound lean pork tenderloin, diced

¼ teaspoon black pepper, freshly ground

1 teaspoon salt

2 cups cooked *udon* noodle

½ cup strained *miso*

1. In large saucepan, boil shrimp and water 15 minutes.
2. Add turnip, onion, pork tenderloin, pepper, salt. Boil for another 10 minutes. Add *udon* noodle and *miso*.
3. Simmer additional 5 minutes over moderate heat.
4. Serve hot.

SERVES 4

Salads

The salads of Asian cuisines range from utterly simple to highly complex. They differ from Western salads in a number of ways, especially in their variety and in the types of dressings they take.

Asian salads are prepared either raw or half cooked. The well-known Indonesian cooked salad, *gado-gado*, is dressed with an unusual but delicious sauce enriched with coconut milk and crushed, crunchy peanuts. The *aemono* salad style of Japan features cooked ingredients; the *sunomono* style uses raw fish, seafood, and vegetables tossed with light vinegar dressing. In the Philippines, the American influence is detected by the presence of a salad at most meals, but with a considerable difference: vegetables are either blanched, boiled, or pickled, and served with a dressing that mingles the flavors of sweet, sour, and salt. A popular accompaniment to Filipino salads is *bagoong*, a salty shrimp paste; another popular dressing is prepared with finely diced tomatoes, onions, ginger, and a whiff of hot pepper. Vietnamese salads contain thinly sliced boiled pork or chicken, mixed with shrimp and julienne-cut radishes and cucumbers, and coated with a thin dressing that has fish sauce as a basic ingredient.

The freshness of vegetables is axiomatic in Asian cookery. Vegetables are never overcooked; they must always retain their crispness and crunchiness. Pickled vegetables must retain their basic colors. The ingredients may vary, the dressings may differ dramatically from one cuisine to another, but this respect for the integrity of ingredients is constant throughout Asian cooking.

Peti Tot

BURMA

(Green Bean Salad)

6 cups salted water for boiling

4 cups fresh green beans

½ teaspoon roasted chili powder

1 medium onion, chopped, fried in 1 tablespoon vegetable oil

2 tablespoons shrimp powder

1 tablespoon fish sauce

2 tablespoons toasted sesame seeds

2 tablespoons vegetable or peanut oil

¼ cup lemon juice

salt to taste

1. Place green beans in boiling salted water and boil 3 minutes.
2. Drain and soak in cold water.
3. Drain beans again and cut diagonally.
4. Place drained beans in a bowl, and add chili, onion, shrimp powder, fish sauce, sesame seeds, oil, and lemon juice. Mix.
5. Add salt to taste and serve chilled.

SERVES 4

Pang Gobi Tot

BURMA

(Cauliflower or Young Collard Greens Salad)

4 cups cauliflower flowerets or young collard greens

salted water for boiling

3 tablespoons vegetable oil

½ teaspoon chili powder

2 cups chopped tomatoes

5 tablespoons powdered roasted peanuts

3 tablespoons lime or lemon juice

salt to taste

1. In boiling salted water, cook cauliflower 4 minutes.
2. Remove cauliflower from heat and immediately immerse in cold water. Drain well, cut into bite-size pieces, and place in salad bowl.
3. In saucepan, heat vegetable oil and fry chili powder. Cool and transfer to salad bowl.
4. Mix well. Add chopped tomatoes, powdered roasted peanuts, and lime or lemon juice. Salt to taste.

SERVES 4

Keyandi Atot

BURMA

(Eggplant Salad)

2 medium eggplants

½ cup scallions, finely minced

1 medium onion, sliced

2 green chilies, finely minced

2 tablespoons peanut or vegetable oil

1 teaspoon fish sauce

salt to taste

1. Broil eggplants until tender (about 20 minutes). Turn until all parts are tender.
2. Remove the skins and place eggplants in salad bowl.
3. Combine scallions, onion, green chilies, oil, and fish sauce with eggplant. Mix well. Add salt to taste.

SERVES 4

Thanatsone

BURMA

(Mixed Vegetable Salad)

4 cups sliced (bite-size) vegetables: (cabbages, cauliflower, carrots, okra, scallions, zucchini, or bean sprouts may be used)

salted water for boiling

1 tablespoon salt

1½ tablespoons sesame oil

½ cup vegetable oil

½ teaspoon ground turmeric

2 cups onion, finely minced

6 garlic cloves, finely minced

3 tablespoons cider vinegar

salt and pepper to taste

4 tablespoons sesame seeds, toasted

1. Drop vegetables in boiling salted water and boil 2 minutes. Drain in colander and arrest the cooking process by running cold water over vegetables. Drain well and set aside.
2. In frying pan, combine sesame and vegetable oils. Heat over medium heat. Add turmeric, onions, and garlic. Sauté until onions are transparent. Set aside to cool.
3. Place cooled vegetables in a salad bowl. Pour mixture over the vegetables. Add cider vinegar and salt and pepper to taste.
4. Serve the vegetables sprinkled with toasted sesame seeds.

SERVES 4

Yum Yai

THAILAND

(Multiflavored Salad)

- 1 8-ounce beef sirloin or flank steak
- 2 tablespoons lime or lemon juice
- 1 fresh green chili pepper, shredded
- 1 tablespoon fish sauce
- 1 medium cucumber, sliced thinly
- 1 hardboiled egg, sliced
- 8 lettuce leaves
- 2 medium tomatoes, sliced
- 2 tablespoons fresh coriander, chopped

1. Broil the steak, or grill over hot charcoal, until medium rare.
2. Cut into thin slices and mix with lemon juice, chili pepper, and fish sauce.
3. Arrange beef with cucumber, egg slices, lettuce leaves, and tomato slices on a large platter. Garnish with fresh coriander.

SERVES 4

Paht Toouh Ngawk Gap Dow Hoo

THAILAND

(Bean Sprouts with Bean Curd)

- 8 ounces fresh bean curd cakes, cut in 1-inch cubes
- 1½ cups vegetable oil
- 2 teaspoons garlic, finely minced
- 6 ounces fresh bean sprouts
- ½ cup scallions, minced
- ¼ teaspoon sugar
- 2 tablespoons fish sauce

1. Heat oil in a deep frying pan and when very hot, fry bean curd cakes until golden brown (about 5 minutes). Drain on paper towel and set aside.
2. Pour off oil from pan and stir-fry garlic and bean sprouts 1 minute.
3. Add scallions, sugar, and fish sauce and continue to stir-fry for another minute.
4. Place bean curd cubes on a dish and cover with mixture.
5. Serve immediately.

SERVES 4

Kong Namul

KOREA

(Bean Sprout Salad)

1 pound fresh bean sprouts

Water for boiling

Dressing:

½ teaspoon garlic, finely minced

3 tablespoons soy sauce

1 tablespoon vegetable oil

1 tablespoon sesame oil

1 tablespoon toasted sesame seeds, crushed

⅛ teaspoon chili powder

1 teaspoon sugar

½ cup scallions, finely minced

1. Drop fresh bean sprouts in boiling water. As soon as the water returns to the boil, remove the sprouts and immediately run under cold water. Drain sprouts and set aside.
2. Combine all the dressing ingredients in a mixing bowl. Mix well.
3. Add bean sprouts to dressing and toss well. Chill before serving.

SERVES 4

Mu Saingchai

KOREA

(White Radish Salad)

3 white radishes, peeled and cut julienne style

2 green apples, peeled and cut julienne style

¼ cup lemon juice

¾ cup scallions, finely minced

Dressing:

3 teaspoons sugar

1 teaspoon salt

3 teaspoons sesame oil

1 tablespoon vegetable oil

3 tablespoons soy sauce

3 tablespoons cider vinegar

1 tablespoon toasted sesame seeds, crushed

1 fresh hot red chili, seeded and finely minced

1. Soak radishes and apples in cold water with lemon juice.
2. Combine all dressing ingredients in a mixing bowl. Mix well.
3. Toss drained apples, radishes, and scallions. Mix with dressing and chill before serving.

SERVES 4

Asinan

INDONESIA

(Cucumber Salad with Sweet and Sour Dressing)

4 cucumbers, seeded, cut julienne-style

1 cup onion, finely minced

1 fresh red chili pepper, seeded, thinly sliced

Dressing:

½ teaspoon garlic powder

¼ cup cider vinegar

2 teaspoons brown sugar

½ teaspoon salt

¼ cup vegetable oil

1. Combine cucumbers, onion, and pepper in a salad bowl.
2. Add the dressing to the salad bowl and mix well.
3. Refrigerate overnight. Serve chilled.

SERVES 4

Gado Gado

INDONESIA

(Salad with Peanut Dressing)

- 1 cup carrots, cut julienne-style and cut in half again
- 4 cups cucumber, seeded, cut in thin slices
- 2 cups cabbage, cut julienne-style and cut in half again (spinach or shredded lettuce may be substituted.)
- ½ pound fresh bean sprouts, washed and drained
- ½ pound green beans, cut in 2-inch pieces

Dressing:

- 4 tablespoons vegetable oil
- ½ cup onion, finely minced
- 1 teaspoon ground chili powder
- 1 teaspoon sugar
- 1 cup water
- 1 tablespoon cider vinegar
- ½ cup crunchy-style peanut butter
- salt to taste

1. Blanch vegetables, rinse immediately in cold water, and drain.
2. Place vegetables in large salad bowl.
3. In a frying pan, sauté onion in oil until transparent. Add remaining dressing ingredients to pan and sauté, stirring until they become a smooth paste (about 5 minutes). Simmer another 2 minutes. Cool to room temperature.
4. Pour dressing on top of vegetables in salad bowl.

Serves 6

Kyabetsu Goma

JAPAN

(Cabbage with Sesame Dressing)

1 medium cabbage, finely shredded

4 cups water

½ tablespoon salt

3 tablespoons ground sesame seeds

6 tablespoons soy sauce

3 tablespoons sugar

½ teaspoon salt

1. In large saucepan, cook cabbage in water and salt until tender (about 5 minutes).
2. Drain well. Gently squeeze water carefully from cabbage.
3. Combine ground sesame seeds, soy sauce, sugar, and salt in mixing bowl. Mix well.
4. Add cabbage to mixture and toss lightly.
5. Serve warm.

SERVES 6

Horenso No Goma-Ae

JAPAN

(Spinach and Sesame Seed Salad)

1 pound fresh spinach, thoroughly washed and drained, with tough stems removed

6 cups water

½ tablespoon salt

2 tablespoons roasted white sesame seeds

2 tablespoons soy sauce

1 tablespoon sugar

¼ teaspoon salt

2 tablespoons vegetable oil

2 tablespoons white vinegar

1. In large saucepan, boil water and salt. Add spinach and continue to boil 1 minute. Drain and rinse in cold water. Drain again and squeeze excess water carefully from spinach.
2. Combine sesame seeds, soy sauce, sugar, salt, vegetable oil, and white vinegar in a mixing bowl. Mix well.
3. Place spinach in bowl and pour the mixture onto spinach. Let stand 2 hours.
4. Serve at room temperature.

SERVES 4

Tsukemono

JAPAN

(Pickled Mixed Vegetables)

1 large eggplant, cut in thin slices

2 medium cucumbers, cut in thin slices

3 carrots, peeled, cut in thin slices

3 medium turnips, peeled and cut in thin slices

5 tablespoons salt

soy sauce

1. Clean and wash vegetables.
2. Place vegetables layer by layer in a glass jar. Alternate layers of vegetables. Sprinkle salt on each layer.
3. Cover jar with plate or wooden lid slightly smaller than the diameter of the opening. Place heavy weight on top of cover.
4. Let stand 4 days. When water from vegetables has risen to the top of the jar, the dish is ready to serve.
5. Serve with soy sauce at room temperature.

SERVES 4–6

Rice

The heart of any Asian meal is rice. It may be simply boiled in water, or served with a dash of salt and pure coconut milk. Frying extends the life of a pot of rice boiled the day before; garnished bountifully with bits of meat, fish, or vegetable leftovers, or spiced with a variety of herbs, seasonings, and food colors, fried rice adds a dash of exotic taste or color to a meal. Rice can be the beginning and the end of any meal, tying together the appetizers, soups, main dishes, salads, and savories to the ultimate course—dessert.

Many Asians love to eat their rice simply cooked, and cooking this staple is an art. Growing it is an act of reverence to nature. With Thailand as its birthplace, rice is a true native of Asia. Rice symbolizes all food, all good omens, as well as fertility and success. Its presence in any Asian meal is obligatory. Rice is called "the bread of life," and the Thai word for dining literally means "to eat rice."

Tradition demands a thick steel pan for cooking rice. However, the electric rice cooker is now a common substitute. Rice cookers imported from Japan are available in most department stores and Oriental food stores.

As a culinary experience, the *rijstafels*, or rice banquets, of Indonesia are a must. Thais love rice with little rolls of pork dipped in a hot sauce. The *nonya* cooks of Singapore prepare rice with lentils, garlic, and other spices.

The eminent food scholar Waverley Root has referred to rice as "the food of enormous populations," and has observed that in the Philippines, "you can stuff your guests with food, but if there is no rice it is not considered that you have offered them a meal." In China, there is a saying which goes, "a meal without rice is like a beautiful girl with only one eye." To the Oriental, an existence without rice is irreparably flawed.

With dishes based on rice, Asian cooks have built a parliament of flavors, an expression of this bounteous grain's infinite variety. Included in this chapter are rice dishes that feature recipes for all occasions and types of meals.

Shanghai Fried Rice

THE PHILIPPINES

(Philippine Shanghai-Style Fried Rice)

- 2 tablespoons garlic, finely minced
- ¼ cup shallots, finely minced
- 4 tablespoons vegetable oil
- 3 Chinese sausages, sliced into ⅛-inch-thick pieces
- ½ cup pork loin, finely sliced
- ½ cup fresh shrimps, chopped (without shells)
- 3 tablespoons soy sauce
- ¼ cup parsley, finely chopped
- 5 cups cold cooked rice mashed lightly with 1 cup of cold water
- ¼ cup scallions

1. In 10- or 12-inch frying pan, fry garlic and shallots in oil.
2. Add sausages, pork, and shrimps. Add soy sauce and parsley.
3. Add rice. Continue frying and turning 10 minutes, blending all ingredients.
4. Serve hot, garnished with scallions.

SERVES 8

Kaning Puti

THE PHILIPPINES

(Boiled Rice)

2 cups raw white rice
4 cups water
dash of salt

1. In heavy saucepan, wash rice two or three times and drain.
2. Add water and salt.
3. Bring to boil and simmer about 15 minutes or until rice is cooked.

SERVES 4

Shwe Htamin

BURMA

(Golden Rice)

1 cup long-grain rice
1½ tablespoons vegetable oil
¼ teaspoon ground turmeric
1 8-ounce can coconut milk

1. Heat oil in skillet and fry rice 5 minutes. Stir constantly.
2. Add turmeric and coconut milk and simmer covered 15 minutes.
3. Serve hot.

SERVES 4

Ohn Htamin

BURMA

(Coconut Rice)

2 cups raw white rice

1 12-ounce can coconut milk

2 small onions, quartered

1 tablespoon vegetable oil

½ tablespoon salt

¼ teaspoon turmeric

2 whole cloves

½ stick cinnamon

2 bay leaves

1. In heavy saucepan, combine rice, coconut milk, onions, oil, salt, turmeric, cloves, cinnamon, and bay leaves. Mix well.
2. Bring to a boil and simmer about 15 minutes, or until rice is cooked.

SERVES 4

Kao Pad

THAILAND

(Thai Fried Rice)

3 tablespoons vegetable oil

1 cup onion, minced

2 teaspoons garlic, finely minced

½ pound lean pork, diced

3 cups cold cooked rice

2 tablespoons fish sauce

1 ripe tomato, chopped

½ cup scallions, finely minced

1 green bell pepper, finely chopped

2 tablespoons water

3 eggs, beaten

1 tablespoon fresh coriander, chopped

1. In a large pan, sauté onion and garlic in oil until onion turns translucent.
2. Add pork and stir-fry until tender (about 4 minutes).
3. Add cooked rice, fish sauce, tomato, scallions, green bell pepper, and water. Cook over moderate heat, stirring well, until warmed through. Cover and cook 2 minutes more.
4. Pour in beaten eggs and coriander. Stir well.
5. Serve immediately.

SERVES 4

Kao Pad Gai

THAILAND

(Fried Rice with Chicken)

3 tablespoons vegetable oil

3 teaspoons garlic, finely minced

1 cup bean curd, cut into ½-inch cubes

1 medium chicken breast, cut in thin strips

½ pound lean pork, cut in thin strips

1 teaspoon dried shrimp powder

1 teaspoon red chili powder

2 tablespoons fish sauce

3 cups cold cooked rice

juice of 1 lemon

2 tablespoons coriander leaves, chopped

2 eggs, beaten and fried as omelette, cut in thin strips

1. In large saucepan, heat oil and fry garlic until golden in color.
2. Add bean curd. Cook until brown.
3. Pour in chicken and pork strips and stir-fry until done (about 8 minutes).
4. Add shrimp powder, red chili powder, fish sauce, and rice. Continue stirring 3 minutes. Squeeze in lemon juice and mix well.
5. Transfer to a large platter, and garnish with coriander leaves and fried egg strips.

SERVES 4

Song-I Bahb

KOREA

(Mushrooms with Rice)

2 tablespoons vegetable oil

1½ cups onion, minced

8 ounces fresh mushrooms, sliced

1 cup lean steak, finely shredded

1 pound rice

3 cups hot water

1 teaspoon salt

½ teaspoon ground black pepper

3 teaspoons soy sauce

3 tablespoons toasted ground sesame seeds

1. Heat oil in large saucepan. Fry onions, mushrooms, and steak 3 minutes.
2. Add rice, hot water, salt, black pepper, soy sauce, and sesame seeds. Bring to boil.
3. Cover and cook 30 minutes.
4. Serve hot.

Serves 6

Bokum Bahb

KOREA

(Crab and Pork Fried Rice)

3 tablespoons vegetable oil

¾ cup cooked crab meat, flaked

1 tablespoon garlic, finely minced

1 tablespoon fresh ginger, finely minced

¾ cup cooked pork, chopped

5 cups cooked rice

1 teaspoon salt

½ cup scallions, finely minced

1. Heat oil in large frying pan. Add crab meat, garlic, ginger, pork, rice, and salt.
2. Stir-fry until rice is golden brown.
3. Add scallions and serve hot.

SERVES 6

Nasi Goreng

INDONESIA

(Fried Rice)

3 eggs

4 tablespoons vegetable oil

1 clove garlic, finely minced

2 fresh red chilies

1 cup onion, finely minced

¾ teaspoon shrimp paste

1 cup cooked meat (beef, ham, pork, or chicken), diced

1 cup cooked shrimp, peeled and deveined

3 cups cooked rice

2 tablespoons dark soy sauce

1 cup cucumber slices

1. Beat eggs to prepare and cook as an omelette. When cooked, let cool and cut julienne-style. Set aside.
2. In saucepan, place 1 teaspoon oil and sauté garlic, red chilies, and onion for 5 minutes. Add shrimp paste, meat, and shrimp. Mix well.
3. Continue to mix well and heat through. Add rice and dark soy sauce and stir-fry 15 minutes.
4. Transfer mixture to large platter and place omelette strips on top.
5. Arrange cucumber slices around edge of platter.

SERVES 4–6

Nasi Kuning

INDONESIA

(Yellow Rice)

- ½ pound rice (washed thoroughly, until water runs clear)
- water
- ¾ teaspoon turmeric
- ½ teaspoon *laos* powder
- 2 curry leaves
- 1¼ cups coconut milk

1. Place rice in covered saucepan. Cover rice with water (water should be 1 inch above rice). Boil until water is *almost* evaporated.
2. In separate saucepan, bring to boil turmeric, *laos* powder, curry leaves, and coconut milk. Pour the rice into this mixture.
3. Cook uncovered, over low heat, about 40 minutes, stirring occasionally, until all liquid has evaporated and steam is escaping through the surface of the rice.
4. Serve hot.

SERVES 6

Nasi Gurith

INDONESIA

(Coconut Rice)

2 cups white rice

1 curry leaf

salt to taste

1 1-inch stem lemon grass (or 1 teaspoon lemon peel or lime peel)

3 cups coconut milk

1. Wash rice several times until water is clear.
2. In large covered saucepan, combine curry leaf, salt, lemon grass, and coconut milk. Bring to a boil.
3. Add rice and continue boiling about 10 minutes. When liquid is almost evaporated, lower heat and cover. Let simmer about 20 minutes longer.
4. Turn heat off and leave covered another 10 minutes.
5. Serve hot.

SERVES 4

Bay Poun

CAMBODIA and LAOS

(Molded Rice)

- ½ cup pork fat, chopped
- ½ cup lean pork, chopped
- 2 tablespoons garlic, finely minced
- ½ cup scallions, finely minced
- ½ cup chicken meat, chopped
- 4 cups hot cooked rice
- 1 teaspoon fish sauce
- ¼ teaspoon freshly ground black pepper

1. In large saucepan, fry pork fat until golden. Add pork, garlic, scallions, and chicken meat. Stir-fry until meat is cooked.
2. Add cooked rice, fish sauce, and pepper. Mix well.
3. Press into a large mold or individual soup or coffee cups. Turn out and serve.

SERVES 4

Com Chien

VIETNAM

(Pot Fried Rice)

1½ tablespoons butter

2 cloves garlic, finely minced

2½ cups raw rice

1 teaspoon salt

2½ cups boiling water

1. In cooking pot with a tight lid, melt butter and sauté garlic 3 minutes.
2. Add rice and salt. Stir-fry until rice turns golden.
3. Pour boiling water into pot, mix, and cover. Cook over low heat 10 minutes.
4. Serve when rice is done (soft).

SERVES 4–6

Noodles

Noodles are an ancient ingredient in Oriental cuisine. Originating in China, they spread rapidly to the tables of the rest of Asia. Marco Polo claimed to have eaten noodles at the court of Kubla Khan in fabled Cathay. On the island of Sumatra, now a part of Indonesia, he tasted a kind of lasagna which he noted was made from breadfruit flour.

Noodles, which have a variety of names in the languages of the region, are usually translucent, finely cut sticks or paper-thin squares. Mostly gelatinous, they are made from ingredients that differ often considerably from the durum wheat pastas of Europe. The rice-stick noodles of China and the Philippines are made from rice flours, while buckwheat flour is the ingredient of the sweet-sour Japanese noodles. White wheat flour is made into egg noodles and a noodle that closely resembles Italian spaghetti. Mung-bean starch is made into cellophane noodles; potato starch is the basis of the *harusane* and *sai fun* noodles of Japan. Starch from acorns is used to make the Korean noodles known for their delectable nutty flavor.

Prepared differently from Western-style pasta, Asian noodles are softened first in either hot or cold water and then briefly cooked in mixtures of fried or simmered ingredients. When prepared in this manner, the noodles expand in size and become pliable and chewy. They are added to soups for body and texture, and to other dishes for textural interest as well as flavor.

Noodle dishes are either dry, with just a touch of sauce, or brothy. When served dry and sautéed with vegetables, thin slices of meat, or seafood, they resemble the pasta dishes of the West. When brothy, they are similar to the Vietnamese favorite known as *pho*, a soup dish of noodles, thin slices of meat, and sprinklings of spring onions and fresh bean sprouts, all blended with the juices extracted from seafood.

Asians regard noodles as a symbol of long life and good health. When served in dishes created to make use of local or seasonal ingredients and to provide an alternate to rice, they offer a message of goodwill, a gesture of wishing well to others.

Char Kway Teow

MALAYSIA

(Fried Rice Noodles)

- 5 tablespoons vegetable oil
- 2 teaspoons garlic, finely minced
- 3 fresh red chilies, seeded and finely sliced
- 1½ cups onions, sliced
- 8 ounces small raw prawns, shelled and deveined
- 4 ounces barbecued pork, thinly sliced
- 2 Chinese sausages, cut diagonally in thin pieces
- 1½ cups fresh bean sprouts
- 2 pounds fresh rice noodles (*kway teow*), cut in strips
- 3 tablespoons soy sauce
- 1 tablespoon oyster sauce
- 3 eggs, beaten
- ⅛ teaspoon freshly ground pepper
- salt to taste
- 1 cup scallions, finely minced

1. Heat 2 tablespoons oil in a large skillet, and fry garlic, chilies, and onions until golden brown and transparent. Stir.
2. Add prawns, pork, and sausages, and continue stirring 5 minutes.
3. Drop bean sprouts into mixture. Cook, stirring, 1 minute, then remove mixture from pan.
4. Heat remaining oil in skillet. Add rice noodles. Stir-fry 3 minutes. Add soy sauce and oyster sauce, continue stirring. Pour beaten eggs into mixture and stir well.
5. Add salt to taste and fresh ground pepper.
6. Add meat and prawn mixture to the skillet.
7. Transfer to a large serving platter. Garnish with scallions.

SERVES 6

Solong Tang

KOREA

(Beef Soup with Noodles and Ginger)

¼ pound fresh wheat noodles

water for boiling

4 cups beef stock

2 teaspoons salt

¾ cup scallions, finely minced

2 teaspoons fresh ginger root, finely minced

1 teaspoon sugar

2 teaspoons ground black pepper

1½ pound cooked beef brisket, cut in paper-thin slices, 2 inches long, ½ inch wide

1. Bring water to a boil. Drop noodles into water, and boil 5 minutes. Drain and set aside.
2. In a large saucepan, bring to boil beef stock, salt, minced scallions, ginger root, sugar, and pepper.
3. Add beef to mixture and simmer 5 minutes.
4. Place noodles in a large soup bowl. Pour beef stock mixture over noodles.
5. Top with sliced beef brisket.
6. Serve hot.

SERVES 4

Khoua Kai Sai Khao Poon Chin

LAOS

(Fried Chicken with Chinese Vermicelli)

- 1 chicken (2–3 pounds), cut in serving pieces
- ½ teaspoon salt
- ½ teaspoon freshly ground pepper
- 2 teaspoons garlic, finely crushed
- 2 tablespoons vegetable oil
- 3 dried red chili peppers, soaked in water until soft
- 5 shallots, finely minced
- 1 cup onion, chopped
- 4 teaspoons lime juice
- 1 teaspoon fish sauce
- 1 16-ounce can coconut milk
- 2 cups soaked Chinese vermicelli
- ½ cup scallions, finely minced

1. Rub chicken with salt, pepper, and garlic. Set aside.
2. Pound chili and shallots into paste-like consistency.
3. Heat oil in large saucepan. Fry chili and shallot paste.
4. Add chicken, onion, lime juice, and fish sauce. Continue frying 10 minutes. Stir well.
5. Add coconut milk and vermicelli and simmer 15 minutes longer.
6. Serve hot. Garnish with minced scallions.

SERVES 4

Kai Keng Khao Poon Chin

LAOS

(Hot Chicken Soup with Chinese Vermicelli)

- 7 cups water
- ½ teaspoon salt
- ½ cup scallions, chopped
- 3 bunches coriander roots
- 1 chicken (2–3 pounds)
- 1 teaspoon fish sauce
- 6 shallots, peeled
- 4 tablespoons Chinese jelly mushrooms, washed, soaked, and sliced
- 4 large potatoes, peeled and cut in ½-inch cubes
- ½ pound Chinese vermicelli, soaked and cut up
- 2 eggs, beaten, fried as an omelette, and cut in thin strips
- ½ cup scallions, finely minced
- ½ teaspoon freshly ground pepper
- ½ cup coriander leaves, finely chopped

1. Boil 7 cups of water in large saucepan. Add salt, chopped scallions, coriander roots, and chicken. Continue to boil until chicken is done. Let cool. Strain stock. Set aside. Remove bones and skin from chicken and shred chicken meat. Set aside.
2. Return strained stock to pot and bring to a boil. Add fish sauce, shallots, and mushrooms. Simmer 10 minutes.
3. Add potatoes, shredded chicken meat, and vermicelli. Simmer for 10 minutes.
4. Transfer to large serving bowl and garnish with egg strips, minced scallions, pepper, and coriander leaves.
5. Serve hot.

SERVES 6

Tsukimi Udon

JAPAN

(Noodles with Broth)

1 pound *udon*

water for boiling

4 cups *dashi*

1 tablespoon sugar

1½ teaspoons salt

1 tablespoon soy sauce

4 eggs

½ cup scallions, finely minced

5 inch square piece of *nori* (purple laver seaweed)

1. Boil *udon* in water until done (al dente). Drain and rinse thoroughly in cold water. Set aside.
2. In large saucepan, boil *dashi*, sugar, salt, and soy sauce. Add noodles. Stir frequently.
3. Place broth in 4 individual soup bowls. Break 1 egg into each bowl.
4. Garnish with scallions and *nori* shreds.
5. Cover soup bowls with lids.
6. Serve hot.

SERVES 4

Tien Mein Tongku

CHINA

(Soft Fried Noodles with Mushrooms)

- 8 ounces egg noodles, boiled until al dente and drained
- 3 tablespoons vegetable oil
- 1 cup almonds, sliced
- 1 cup bamboo shoots, sliced
- ¾ cup chicken broth
- 3 tablespoons soy sauce
- ⅛ teaspoon freshly ground black pepper

1. In large frying pan, heat oil over low heat and add egg noodles. Stir-fry 5 minutes.
2. Add mushrooms, almonds, bamboo shoots, chicken broth, soy sauce, and ground pepper. Mix thoroughly. Cover and cook 15 minutes more.
3. Serve hot.

SERVES 4

Soyuk Tien Mein

CHINA

(Ground Meat with Bean Noodles)

- 8 ounces ground pork
- 1 teaspoon salt
- 1 tablespoon soy sauce
- 1 tablespoon dry sherry
- 2 cups vegetable oil
- 1 stick Chinese sausage, diced
- 2 red chili peppers, diced
- 6 water chestnuts, diced
- ½ cup scallions, finely minced
- 4 ounces bean noodles

1. Marinate pork with salt, soy sauce, and dry sherry for 30 minutes.
2. Heat 1 tablespoon vegetable oil in large frying pan. Add pork. Stir-fry pork until done, about 5 minutes.
3. Add Chinese sausage, pepper, chestnuts, and scallions. Stir well for 3 minutes. Set mixture aside.
4. Clean pan. Add remaining vegetable oil and deep-fry bean noodles until almost transparent.
5. Transfer noodles onto large serving plate, pressing them to make them flat. Pour meat over noodles and serve hot.

SERVES 4

Jahp Wui Chow Min

CHINA

(Chow Mein)

- 8 ounces fine egg noodles
- 2 cups plus 2 tablespoons vegetable oil
- 1 tablespoon garlic, finely minced
- ¾ cup onion, minced
- 1 teaspoon fresh ginger root, finely grated
- 1 pound cooked pork, diced
- 2 cups cooked chicken, diced
- 1 cup celery, finely chopped
- 1 cup mushrooms, thinly sliced
- 2 cups fresh bean sprouts
- 1 cup bamboo shoots, finely sliced
- 1 teaspoon flour mixed with 2 tablespoons water
- 2 tablespoons soy sauce
- ¼ teaspoon black pepper, freshly ground

1. Boil egg noodles until al dente. Drain and run under cold water. Spread on paper towel and let dry one hour.
2. In large frying pan, deep-fry dried noodles in 2 cups oil until golden. Discard oil and set noodles aside.
3. Clean frying pan. Add 2 tablespoons vegetable oil. Fry garlic, onion, and ginger root 3 minutes.
4. Add pork, chicken, celery, mushrooms, bean sprouts, and bamboo shoots to pan. Stir-fry 5 minutes.
5. Add flour, soy sauce, and pepper. Mix well and simmer 2 minutes.
6. Place noodles on a serving platter. Pour hot mixture over fried noodles.
7. Serve immediately.

SERVES 6

Paht Thai

THAILAND

(Fried Noodles)

- 2 tablespoons vegetable oil
- 2 teaspoons garlic, finely minced
- 4 ounces pork tenderloin, cut in thin strips
- 6 ounces flat rice noodles, soaked in hot water for 10 minutes and drained
- 3 tablespoons peanuts, roasted and crushed
- 2 tablespoons dried shrimps, soaked in warm water for 10 minutes and drained
- 1 cup bean curd cakes, cut into ½-inch cubes
- 2 teaspoons fish sauce
- ¼ teaspoon chili powder
- 1 teaspoon sugar
- ½ cup scallions, cut in 1-inch-long pieces
- 1 teaspoon rice vinegar
- 1 egg, beaten

Condiments:

- 1 cup fresh bean sprouts
- fresh red or green chili pepper, shredded
- fish sauce
- sugar
- lime wedges
- oriental chili powder

1. Heat oil in large frying pan. Add garlic and pork. Stir-fry 1 minute.
2. Add noodles, peanuts, shrimps, bean curd cubes, fish sauce, chili powder, sugar, scallions, and rice vinegar. Stir-fry over medium heat 3 minutes.
3. Pour in beaten egg. Continue to stir-fry another 1 minute.
4. Transfer to serving platter.
5. Serve with condiments.

SERVES 4

Oh-No Khaukswe

BURMA

(Chicken Curry with Noodles)

- 1 chicken (2–3 pounds)
- 1 tablespoon salt
- ½ teaspoon turmeric
- water
- 5 whole dried chilies
- ½ cup plus 2 tablespoons oil
- 6 ounces dry rice noodles (Thai rice vermicelli)
- ½ cup garlic, finely minced
- 2 cups onion, finely minced
- ⅔ cup flour
- 1 12-ounce can coconut milk
- 2 tablespoons fish sauce

1. Rub chicken with salt and turmeric. In a stockpot, cover chicken with water and bring to a boil. Simmer until done (about 30 minutes). Strain broth and set aside. Remove all meat from the boiled chicken, discard the skin and bones, and cut the meat in thin strips.
2. Soak chilies in water and pound. Add 2 tablespoons oil to skillet. Heat over low flame and fry chilies until oil turns red in color (about 4 minutes). Set aside.
3. In a large pot, heat the remaining oil and deep-fry rice noodles, a portion at a time, until crisp. Remove noodles from oil, reserving the oil, and drain on paper towels. Let cool.

4. Sauté garlic and onion in oil remaining from frying noodles. Add chicken meat and stir-fry 5 minutes. Add the stock. Make a paste from the flour and some water and add to the stock, stirring well until the mixture boils and thickens. Add the coconut milk, fish sauce, and red chili oil. Simmer the mixture a few minutes longer, until blended.
5. To serve, put ½ cup fried noodles in individual soup bowls, ladle chicken curry on top, and add accompaniments as desired.

Accompaniments:

6 ounces dry noodles

5 quarts water

2 tablespoons vegetable oil

½ cup chili powder

3 medium onions, sliced and soaked in water

1 cup scallions, finely minced

8 hard-cooked eggs, sliced

5 lemons or limes

1. Boil water. Drop noodles in boiling water and cook until done. Drain, run under cold water, and drain again. Mix with vegetable oil and serve in a large bowl.
2. Pan-roast chili powder 5 minutes, separate grains, and place in a small dish.
3. Arrange onions, lemons or limes, scallions, and egg slices on a platter.

SERVES 8

Kauskwe Kyaw

BURMA

(Mixed Fried Noodles)

- 1 pound egg noodles
- 5 tablespoons vegetable oil
- 2 cups onions, minced
- 3 tablespoons garlic, finely minced
- 1 pound chicken breast, finely sliced
- 1 chicken liver, finely sliced
- ¼ cup celery, cut julienne style, cut again crosswise
- 1 cup cabbage, cut julienne style, cut again crosswise
- 1 cup Chinese cabbage, cut julienne style, cut again crosswise
- 5 dried Chinese mushrooms, soaked in warm water 1 hour or longer, cut julienne style
- soy sauce
- salt and pepper to taste
- ½ cup finely minced scallions
- 4 eggs, beaten

1. Cook noodles according to package instructions, boiling until tender. Drain and transfer to a large platter. Pour in 2 tablespoons oil, and mix well.
2. Heat 3 tablespoons oil in skillet, add garlic and onions, and sauté until onions are transparent.
3. Add chicken and liver and sauté until tender (about 8 minutes).
4. Add celery, cabbage, mushrooms, and soy sauce to taste, cooking and stirring until crisp but tender (about 8 minutes more). Add salt and pepper to taste.
5. Scramble eggs and use as garnish.

SERVES 8

Sotanghon Bola-Bola

THE PHILIPPINES

(Noodles with Meatballs)

- ½ cup ground pork
- ¼ cup chopped onion
- 1 egg
- 1 tablespoon flour
- 1 tablespoon salt
- ¼ teaspoon pepper
- 2 tablespoons oil
- 3 tablespoons garlic, minced
- 3 tablespoons onion, sliced
- 2 cups chicken or beef broth
- 1½ pounds *sotanghon* (bean-thread noodles), soaked in 1 cup water*
- 2 tablespoons soy sauce
- ¼ cup scallions or green onions, diced

1. Combine pork, onion, egg, flour, salt, and pepper. Mix well and form into balls about 1 inch in diameter.
2. Sauté garlic and onion in oil. Add broth and bring to boil.
3. Add meatballs one at a time, and cook until meat is done.
4. Add *sotanghon* and cook about 10 minutes. Season with soy sauce and more pepper to taste.
5. Sprinkle with scallions or green onions just before serving. Serve hot.

SERVES 4

*Misua (threadlike noodles) or vermicelli can also be used. This is called Bola-Bolang Misua.

Pancit Molo

THE PHILIPPINES

(Philippine Wonton Soup)

Filling:

- 1 cup ground pork
- ½ cup shrimps, shelled, deveined, chopped
- ½ cup onion, finely chopped
- 2 egg yolks
- ¼ cup scallions, finely sliced
- 2 teaspoons garlic, finely minced
- ½ cup water chestnuts, finely minced
- 1 teaspoon salt
- ¼ teaspoon pepper

Combine all ingredients, blend well. Set aside.

Wrapper: (can also be bought ready-made at Oriental food stores)

- 2 cups all-purpose flour
- ¼ teaspoon salt
- 3 egg yolks
- ¼ cup water

1. Sift flour and salt together. Add yolks and knead with fingers.
2. Gradually add water and continue kneading until dough is elastic and smooth. Roll out on a floured board until paper thin.
3. Cut into triangles, with sides of each triangle measuring about 3 inches.
4. Scoop 1 teaspoon filling onto each wrapper and fold two corners in. Fold and press third corner to seal (like a pouch). (When using ready-made wrappers, fold two corners opposite each other and then the two others to seal like a pouch.)

Broth:

- 1 chicken (3 pounds)
- 15 cups water
- 2 tablespoons finely minced garlic
- 1 cup finely chopped onion
- 2 tablespoons vegetable or corn oil
- 1 cup shrimps, shelled and deveined
- fish sauce or salt and freshly ground pepper
- ½ cup finely chopped scallions

1. Boil chicken in water till tender. Remove meat from bones, cut into serving pieces, and set aside chicken and broth.
2. In a large saucepan, sauté garlic and onion in oil. Garlic is done when light brown and onion when transparent.
3. Add the chicken, broth, and shrimps to the sautéed mixture. Season with fish sauce or salt and pepper to taste. Bring to a boil.
4. Drop the wrapped stuffing into the broth and cook for 10 minutes.
5. Garnish with scallions.

SERVES 4

Pancit Mami

THE PHILIPPINES

(Noodles in Broth)

¼ pound lean pork

1 chicken breast, whole

3 cups water

1 teaspoon salt

2 tablespoons vegetable or corn oil

1 tablespoon garlic, finely minced

1 onion, minced

salt and pepper to taste

1 pound fresh *miki* (rice noodles sold in Oriental food stores), or flat, wide egg noodles

2 tablespoons scallions, finely minced

1. In medium pot, boil pork and chicken in 3 cups water. Cook until tender. Season with salt. Remove from water and cool.
2. Cut pork in strips and remove chicken from bone and shred meat. Set aside. Save 2 cups stock.
3. In large skillet, heat oil and sauté garlic and onion. Add pork, chicken, and stock. Simmer two minutes. Season with salt and pepper.
4. Place uncooked *miki* in serving bowls and pour over enough of the chicken-pork broth to fill the bowls (the hot broth will cook the noodles).
5. Garnish each bowl with minced scallions. Serve hot.

SERVES 4

Vegetables

The vegetable cookery of Asia has a great virtue, one which has only recently been widely acknowledged in the West. That is the finely tuned sense of timing in the cooking, so that vegetables come out tender, crisp, and crunchy in texture, while retaining all their original flavor and color.

The vegetarian tradition of Asia is at least as old as Hinduism, which developed in India during the millennium preceding the birth of Christ; Buddhism, itself over a thousand years old, also has a long vegetarian tradition. It is hardly surprising that the preparation of vegetables, which are plentiful in Asia, should have become the culinary art form that it has.

Asians use vegetables in every manner imaginable—as main dishes, in soups, as appetizers and snacks. Vegetables provide not only vital nutrients but also interesting tastes, colors, and an expression of folk artistry. Various preparation techniques such as uniform slicing or carving are observed, and greens are often added just before a dish is removed from the heat. Vegetables are used raw in salads, or preserved to be used as side dishes to accompany meat, fish, and poultry.

Among the great delicacies of Asian cuisine are the many varieties of mushroom. When dried, the mushroom becomes a most versatile and long-lasting ingredient in hundreds of different preparations. The Japanese *shiitake* is the most popular and one of the most delicious of dried mushrooms.

The radish, which is native to Asia, is by far the most versatile vegetable. It is used in salads, as a garnish, in main dishes; the seeds are dried, treated, and pressed to yield an oil which is highly valued by Chinese gourmets.

Picking vegetables at dawn and using them at once is the secret of Asia's superior vegetable cookery. The food markets of Asia burgeon with fresh vegetables grown in home gardens or on small farms, for Asians are born gardeners.

Com Xao Rau

VIETNAM

(Mixed Vegetables, Vietnamese Style)

- 2 tablespoons vegetable oil
- 1 cup broccoli flowerets (or cauliflower)
- 1 cup turnip, shredded
- 1 cup carrots, shredded
- 1 cup celery, cut julienne style
- 1 cup leeks, cut julienne style (or 1 small onion)
- 2½ tablespoons fish sauce or soy sauce
- ¼ teaspoon Five Spice powder (or clove or pepper)

1. In large frying pan or wok, heat oil and stir-fry the vegetables in the following order: broccoli, turnip, carrots, celery, and leek.
2. Continue stirring 6 minutes. Add fish sauce and Five Spice powder. Stir mixture another 3 minutes.
3. Serve immediately.

Serves 4–6

Lumpia

THE PHILIPPINES

(Vegetable Spring Roll)

Filling:

- 2 tablespoons vegetable oil for sautéing
- 1 tablespoon garlic, finely minced
- ½ cup onion, finely minced
- ½ pound pork, chopped
- ½ cup shrimp, shelled, deveined, chopped
- 2 cups chicken broth
- 1 cup cabbage, finely shredded
- 4 carrots, diced
- 3 medium potatoes, diced
- 1 sweet potato, diced
- ¼ pound green beans, sliced diagonally
- 2 cups boiled chick peas
- 2 tablespoons soy sauce

1. Heat oil in pan and sauté garlic until light brown. Add onion. When onion is transparent, add pork, shrimp, and broth. Simmer 20 minutes.
2. Add cabbage, carrots, potatoes, sweet potato, green beans, chick peas, and soy sauce. Cook until tender.
3. Set aside and cool.

Wrappers:

3 eggs

2 tablespoons vegetable or corn oil

1 cup cornstarch

1½ cups water

14 lettuce leaves

2 tablespoons parsley, finely chopped

1 cup peanuts, finely crushed

1. Thoroughly beat eggs. Add oil.
2. Stir in cornstarch and salt, stir until dissolved. Add water, mix well.
3. Heat omelette pan. Pour in thin coating of batter to make egg roll. Set aside.
4. Repeat until you have 14 or more wrappers.
5. Spread wrappers on flat surface and line each with lettuce leaf.
6. Put 3 tablespoons filling on each wrapper. Sprinkle with parsley and ground peanuts before sealing.
7. Make roll by folding one side of wrapper to seal in the filling, leaving one side open so that lettuce leaf is visible.
8. Before serving, top with Lumpia Sauce.

Sauce:

½ cup sugar

2 cups water

3 tablespoons soy sauce

3½ teaspoons salt

⅛ teaspoon pepper, freshly ground

2 tablespoons cornstarch

1. Combine all ingredients in saucepan.
2. Cook over high heat, stirring constantly, until sauce thickens.
3. Remove, let cool.
4. Top vegetable spring rolls with sauce.

SERVES 4–6

Bulanglang

THE PHILIPPINES

(Boiled Vegetables)

½ cup onion, quartered

2 tomatoes, chopped

1½ teaspoons shrimp paste

1 cup butternut squash, cubed

1 cup water

1 cup bean curd, sliced and fried

1 cup zucchini, sliced

½ pound spinach

1. Combine onion, tomatoes, shrimp paste, and squash in deep saucepan.
2. Add water and bring to boil.
3. Add bean curd and zucchini. Simmer until zucchini is tender.
4. Add spinach and cook for another 3 minutes. Serve hot.

SERVES 4

Laing

THE PHILIPPINES

(Spinach with Coconut Milk)

1 pound spinach

1½ cups coconut milk

1½ teaspoons salt

1 teaspoon ginger root, minced

½ cup pork, diced

½ cup shrimp, diced

½ cup coconut cream

2 hot green peppers

1. Chop spinach leaves into bite-size pieces. Set aside.
2. In saucepan, combine coconut milk, salt, ginger, and pork. Simmer until meat is cooked. Add shrimp and simmer 5 minutes longer.
3. Add coconut cream, hot peppers, and spinach. Simmer an additional 3 minutes. Serve hot.

SERVES 4

Rellenong Talong

THE PHILIPPINES

(Stuffed Eggplant)

2 medium eggplants, halved lengthwise

2 eggs, beaten

2 tablespoons cooking oil

1 teaspoon garlic, finely minced

½ cup onion, finely minced

1 pound ground pork or beef

3 ripe tomatoes, chopped

fish sauce or salt and pepper to taste

1 cup bread crumbs

3 tablespoons vegetable or corn oil

1. Broil eggplants, skin side up, until tender. Let cool.
2. Scoop out pulp and reserve for another use. Reserve skin. Soak skin in beaten eggs.
3. In skillet, heat oil and sauté garlic until brown, onion until transparent.
4. Add pork or beef and cook until brown.
5. Add tomatoes and fish sauce or salt and pepper to taste.
6. Continue stirring mixture until it thickens slightly. Remove from heat.
7. Divide stuffing mixture in 4 portions and fill the four eggplant skins with it. Press to make firm. Coat each with bread crumbs and beaten eggs.
8. Heat oil. Fry eggplants on each side until golden brown.

SERVES 4

Ensaladang Pilipino

THE PHILIPPINES

(Philippine Salad)

1 head romaine lettuce, leaves separated and cut in serving pieces

1 cup vinaigrette sauce

5 salted eggs* (see recipe p. 18), peeled and coarsely chopped

5 medium tomatoes, cut in small wedges

1. Line a salad platter with lettuce leaves.
2. Pour ½ cup vinaigrette sauce over lettuce.
3. Arrange tomato slices on lettuce. Top with chopped eggs.
4. Pour remaining vinaigrette sauce over salad and serve.

SERVES 6

Vinaigrette sauce:

½ cup apple cider vinegar

½ teaspoon salt

1 teaspoon sugar

¼ cup water

2 teaspoons parsley, finely minced

1. Combine all ingredients and serve.

YIELD: 1½ CUPS

*Regular hard-cooked eggs may be substituted.

Achara

THE PHILIPPINES

(Relish)

This Indian-influenced melange of sweet-sour relish is a favorite in the Philippines. It is usually eaten as a side dish to accompany fried or broiled fish or meat.

- 1 cup apple cider vinegar
- 1 cup sugar
- 1 tablespoon salt
- 4 cups sauerkraut (or green papaya, cut julienne style)
- 4 cloves garlic, sliced julienne-style, cut in half
- 1 cup carrots, sliced julienne-style, cut in half
- 1 sweet green pepper, cored, seeded, sliced julienne-style
- 1 sweet red pepper, cored, seeded, sliced julienne-style
- ¼ pound ginger root, sliced julienne-style
- 1 cup onion, finely minced
- ½ cup raisins

1. In large saucepan, bring vinegar, sugar, and salt to a boil.
2. Add rest of ingredients, cover, turn off heat. Let cool.
3. Transfer to sterilized jar or bottle.

YIELD: ABOUT 7 CUPS

Pad Tua Ngork

THAILAND

(Fried Bean Sprouts)

- 3 tablespoons vegetable oil
- 3 teaspoons garlic, finely minced
- ½ pound pork tenderloin, sliced thinly, cut into strips ½″ by 2″
- 8 ounces fresh shrimp, shelled and deveined
- ¼ teaspoon black pepper, freshly ground
- 1 teaspoon sugar
- 1½ tablespoons fish sauce
- ½ pound bean sprouts, thoroughly washed and drained

1. In large pan, heat oil and drop in garlic. Cook until golden.
2. Add pork and shrimp, and stir-fry 3 minutes.
3. Season with pepper, sugar, and fish sauce.
4. Add bean sprouts. Stir-fry 3 minutes longer.
5. Serve immediately.

SERVES 4

Paht Pahk

THAILAND

(Stir-Fried Vegetables)

- 2 tablespoons vegetable oil
- 1 teaspoon garlic, finely minced
- 1 cup celery, sliced
- 1 cup bamboo shoots, sliced
- 1 cup snow peas
- 1 cup fresh mushrooms
- ¼ teaspoon black pepper, freshly ground
- 2 tablespoons fish sauce
- ¼ teaspoon sugar

1. In large pan, heat oil and drop in garlic. Stir-fry until golden.
2. Add celery, bamboo shoots, peas, mushrooms. Stir thoroughly 4 minutes.
3. Add pepper, fish sauce, and sugar. Continue stirring 3 minutes or longer, until well blended.
4. Serve immediately.

SERVES 4

Sai Lan

CHINA

(Stir-Fried Broccoli)

- 2 tablespoons peanut oil
- ½ teaspoon salt
- 1 teaspoon fresh ginger root, finely minced
- 1 pound broccoli, separate flowerets, cut stems diagonally, about ⅛ inch thick
- 2 tablespoons sugar
- 3 teaspoons soy sauce
- 1 tablespoon dry sherry
- ⅛ teaspoon black pepper, freshly ground
- 2 tablespoons water

1. In frying pan, heat oil over high heat. Drop in salt and ginger root. Fry until ginger turns brown, about 1 minute.
2. Add broccoli and stir-fry about 2 minutes more.
3. Add sugar, soy sauce, sherry, pepper, and water. Mix well. Stir-fry about 2 minutes longer.
4. Serve immediately.

SERVES 4

Chow Dau Kok

CHINA

(Quick-Fried String Beans)

- 3 tablespoons peanut oil
- ½ teaspoon fresh ginger root, finely grated
- 1 teaspoon garlic, finely minced
- 1 pound green beans, cut into 2-inch lengths
- 1 teaspoon sesame oil
- 1 tablespoon soy sauce

1. Heat peanut oil in frying pan, add ginger, garlic, and beans. Stir constantly over high heat, 3 minutes.
2. Add sesame oil and soy sauce. Stir and cook 1 minute longer.
3. Serve immediately.

SERVES 4

Chow Sub Gum

CHINA

(Fried Mixed Vegetables)

- 3 tablespoons vegetable oil
- 6 Chinese mushrooms, soaked in warm water 1 hour
- ½ cup bamboo shoots, sliced
- ½ cup carrots, sliced
- ½ cup onion, sliced
- ½ cup cucumber, sliced
- ½ cup celery, sliced
- ½ cup water chestnuts, sliced
- 1 cup bean sprouts
- ½ teaspoon salt
- 1 tablespoon dry sherry
- 1 teaspoon sugar
- 2 tablespoons soy sauce
- ½ cup water
- 1 tablespoon cornstarch mixed with 2 tablespoons water

1. Drain mushrooms, remove and discard stems, and slice caps.
2. Heat oil in frying pan. Stir-fry mushrooms, bamboo shoots, carrots, and onions 1 minute.
3. Add cucumber, celery, and water chestnuts. Stir-fry another minute. Add bean sprouts, salt, sherry, sugar, soy sauce, and water and cornstarch mixture.
4. Mix well. Bring to boil for another minute.
5. Serve hot.

SERVES 6

Taukwa Goreng

MALAYSIA

(Stir-Fried and Baked Bean Curd)

- 2 teaspoons dark soy sauce
- 1 teaspoon garlic, finely minced
- ¾ pound ground pork
- 8 squares soft bean curd
- 1 tablespoon vegetable oil
- ½ cup scallions, finely chopped
- 2 eggs, beaten
- 1 cup celery, chopped
- ⅛ teaspoon pepper
- ⅛ teaspoon salt

1. Combine in mixing bowl soy sauce, garlic, and ground pork. Mix well and set aside.
2. Drain soft bean curd on paper towel. Chop.
3. Heat oil. Stir-fry ground pork mixture. Transfer into the mixing bowl.
4. Add all other ingredients to ground pork and mix well.
5. Transfer to an oven-proof dish and place in 250°F oven 30 minutes.
6. Serve hot.

SERVES 4

Kol Goreng

MALAYSIA

(Fried Cabbage)

- 1 tablespoon vegetable oil
- ¾ cup onion, finely minced
- ¼ pound finely chopped pork
- ¼ pound shrimp, peeled and deveined
- 1 fresh red chili, seeded and finely sliced
- 1 small cabbage, finely shredded
- 2 tablespoons soy sauce

1. In large frying pan, heat oil and sauté onion, pork, shrimp, and chili until cooked (about 8 minutes).
2. Add shredded cabbage and soy sauce. Continue stirring about 15 minutes.
3. Serve hot.

SERVES 4

Sayur Goreng

MALAYSIA

(Stir-Fried Mixed Vegetables)

1 tablespoon garlic, finely minced

½ cup shallots, finely minced

1 cup onion, finely minced

4 tablespoons vegetable oil

5 carrots, sliced and peeled

1 medium size cauliflower, broken in flowerets

1 green bell pepper, sliced

10 miniature (baby) ears of corn, available bottled

¼ pound snow peas

½ cup tomato ketchup

¼ cup chili sauce

salt to taste

⅛ teaspoon black pepper, freshly ground

1. Pound together garlic, shallots, onions into a smooth paste.
2. In large frying pan, heat oil and add pounded garlic, shallots, and onions. Fry until golden brown.
3. Add other vegetables and stir-fry for 8 minutes.
4. Add tomato ketchup, chili sauce, salt, and pepper.
5. Continue stirring another 5 minutes. Serve hot.

SERVES 6

Cindauwan

MALAYSIA

(Assorted Braised Mushrooms)

1 8-ounce can button mushrooms

1 8-ounce can golden mushrooms

1 8-ounce can straw mushrooms

½ cup liquid from the canned mushrooms

3 tablespoons vegetable oil

½ cup cooked ham, thinly sliced

1 cup abalone, thinly sliced

1 cup snow peas

salt and pepper to taste

2 teaspoons Chinese wine

1. Drain all mushrooms and set aside. Save ½ cup of mushroom liquid.
2. Heat oil in saucepan. Sauté ham and abalone 5 minutes.
3. Add mushrooms and snow peas, and season with salt and pepper.
4. Stir-fry 3 more minutes. Add Chinese wine and mushroom liquid.
5. Bring to boil. Serve hot.

SERVES 4

Kim Chee

KOREA

(Pickled Chinese Cabbage)

1 head Chinese cabbage (*bok choy*), shredded

4 tablespoons salt

1 cup scallions, finely minced

3 teaspoons garlic, finely minced

2 teaspoons hot chili powder

1½ tablespoon sugar

1 hard pear, peeled, cored, and grated

1. In mixing bowl, combine Chinese cabbage and salt. Leave overnight.
2. Rinse cabbage under cold running water. Drain and set aside.
3. Mix remaining ingredients together. Combine with the drained Chinese cabbage.
4. Store in a covered jar. Let the mixture blend about 2 days before using.

SERVES 8

Shikumchee

KOREA

(Sweet Spinach with Garlic)

2 pounds fresh spinach leaves, discard the stalks

⅛ teaspoon salt

2 teaspoons sugar

3 tablespoons soy sauce

2 tablespoons sesame seeds

¼ cup scallions, finely minced

1 tablespoon sesame seed oil

1 tablespoon garlic, finely minced

1. Parboil spinach leaves. Drain and chop coarsely. Arrange on serving platter.
2. Combine remaining ingredients in mixing bowl. Mix well.
3. Cover spinach with mixture.
4. Serve hot.

SERVES 4

Semur Terong

INDONESIA

(Steamed Eggplant in Dark Sauce)

- 1 pound eggplant, cut crosswise in ½-inch-thick slices
- 1 egg, beaten
- ¼ teaspoon salt
- 8 tablespoons vegetable oil
- ½ cup finely minced onion
- 1 tablespoon finely minced garlic
- ½ teaspoon salt
- ½ teaspoon sugar
- ¼ teaspoon nutmeg
- 3 tablespoons soy sauce
- ½ teaspoon pepper
- 1 cup beef stock

1. Steam eggplant for 8 minutes. Set aside and let cool.
2. Combine eggs and salt. Dip eggplant into egg mixture and fry on both sides in 6 tablespoons vegetable oil until brown. Set aside.
3. Sauté onion and garlic in remaining oil until onion is transparent. Add salt, sugar, nutmeg, soy sauce, pepper, and stock. Simmer 5 minutes. Add eggplant and cook another 3 minutes.
4. Serve immediately.

SERVES 4

Orak Arik

INDONESIA

(Cabbage Scramble)

- 3 tablespoons vegetable oil
- 1½ tablespoons garlic, finely minced
- 2 tablespoons onion, finely minced
- 1 cup shrimp, shelled, deveined, diced
- ½ teaspoon ground black pepper
- ½ teaspoon salt
- 4 cups cabbage, cut julienne-style, cut again crosswise
- 4 eggs, beaten
- ½ cup scallions, finely minced

1. Pour oil into large skillet. Sauté garlic, onion, shrimp, pepper, and salt until onions are transparent, about 10 minutes.
2. Add cabbage and eggs. Continue stirring about 8 minutes.
3. Serve hot. Garnish with scallions.

SERVES 4

Nameko Sake

JAPAN

(Marinated Mushrooms)

- 3 tablespoons sake
- 2 tablespoons soy sauce
- 2 tablespoons sugar
- 4 tablespoons rice wine vinegar
- 1 teaspoon salt
- ½ cup scallions, finely minced
- 3 dozen small mushroom caps, washed and dried

1. Place sake, soy sauce, sugar, vinegar, salt, and scallions in saucepan. Bring to a boil, reduce heat, and simmer about 10 minutes.
2. Place mushroom caps in a bowl. Pour mixture over mushrooms.
3. Marinate overnight in refrigerator.
4. Drain mushrooms thoroughly before serving.

Serves 6–8

Nasu No Karashi

JAPAN

(Mustard-Pickled Eggplant)

1 medium eggplant, quartered lengthwise, then cut crosswise into ⅛-inch thick slices

4 cups water

1½ tablespoons salt

3 tablespoons sugar

3 tablespoons *mirin*

3 tablespoons soy sauce

1 teaspoon dry mustard

1. Soak eggplant in water and 1 tablespoon salt for 2 hours.
2. In mixing bowl, combine ½ tablespoon salt, sugar, *mirin*, soy sauce, and mustard. Mix well.
3. Pat eggplant dry and arrange in serving bowl. Pour dressing over eggplant. Refrigerate overnight.
4. Serve as salad or appetizer.

SERVES 4

Fish

Fish, to Asians, stands for regeneration, abundance, wealth, and prosperity. Because fish—and other seafood—is plentiful in Asia, it is a popular ingredient of Asian cookery, appearing at almost every meal. Fish is used for soups, snacks and appetizers, main courses. When boiled and combined with vegetables and a souring agent like lemon grass or *kalamansi* (Philippine lime), or enriched with coconut milk, fish is a meal in itself. In many Asian cuisines, fish is grilled, barbecued, deep-fried, or pickled. Dried fish and seafood are prepared in coastal towns and cities and shipped to markets far inland.

Condiments made from fermented fish and seafood are part of the standard culinary repertory of Southeast Asia. Known variously as *patis* in the Philippines, *nuoc mam* in Vietnam, *nam pla* in Thailand, *ngan pya ye* in Burma, fish sauce is used as both a flavoring during the cooking process and as a condiment to be added to taste at the table. Salty and fishy in its pure state, fish sauce takes on less definable characteristics when used during the cooking process, adding a distinctive but not overwhelming savor to stews, salads, barbecued or grilled meat and chicken, and to almost any other type of dish but dessert.

The Chinese have a thousand and one ways to use fish products and foods from the sea. The Japanese are famous for their exquisitely presented platters of raw *sushi* and *sashimi*, and for the delicately battered, deep-fried *tempura*. The Filipinos prepare a wonderful stuffed fish, borrowing techniques and an assortment of ingredients from Spanish and other Mediterranean influences. In Indonesia, fish are generally fried or barbecued, and dishes of this sort are delectable, served with a variety of dipping sauces. In Laos and Cambodia, two of the landlocked countries of Asia, fish is the main source of protein. Cooks of these nations dry or salt fish to prolong their usefulness as culinary ingredients.

Kerrie Ikan

INDONESIA

(Curried Fish)

- 2 cups vegetable oil (for frying)
- 6 fresh fillets (snapper, bluefish, carp, or bass), dredged lightly in flour
- 1 teaspoon ground turmeric
- 1½ teaspoons ground coriander
- ½ teaspoon ground cumin
- ½ teaspoon ground ginger
- 5 cloves garlic
- 1 teaspoon shrimp paste
- ½ teaspoon ground lemon grass (or 2 teaspoons fresh lemon juice)
- 2 tablespoons vegetable oil
- ½ cup onion, finely minced
- 2 cups coconut milk
- 1 teaspoon *sambal badjak*
- ¼ cup fresh lemon juice

1. In frying pan, heat oil and deep-fry floured fish fillets. Drain and set aside.
2. In food processor, combine the turmeric, coriander, cumin, ginger, garlic, shrimp paste, and lemon grass. Blend well until smooth. Set aside.
3. In saucepan, heat 2 tablespoons oil. Sauté onion until transparent (about 5 minutes).
4. Add mixture from food processor, coconut milk, and *sambal badjak*. Simmer over low heat 5 minutes.
5. Add fish fillets. Continue simmering until liquid is reduced by half.
6. Add fresh lemon juice and serve.

SERVES 4

Gun Saengsun

KOREA

(Grilled Fish)

- 2 pounds fish fillets (sole, red snapper, or sea bass)
- 1 tablespoon sesame oil
- 3 tablespoons soy sauce
- ½ teaspoon chili sauce
- 1 teaspoon fresh ginger, finely grated
- 2 teaspoons sugar
- 3 tablespoons toasted, crushed sesame seeds
- 1 teaspoon garlic, finely minced

1. In a mixing bowl, marinate fish fillets with the rest of the ingredients, about 2 hours.
2. Remove fish from marinade and place on broiling rack. Broil fish until done (about 5 minutes on each side), brushing it periodically with marinade.
3. Serve hot.

SERVES 6

Tuigim Saengsun

KOREA

(Fried Fish)

- 8 small fish fillets (sea bass, sole, or red snapper)
- 3 teaspoons sesame oil
- ½ cup scallions, finely minced
- 3 tablespoons soy sauce
- 2 tablespoons toasted, crushed sesame seeds
- ¼ teaspoon ground black pepper
- 4 tablespoons vegetable oil

1. In large bowl, combine fish fillets, sesame oil, scallions, soy sauce, sesame seeds, black pepper. Let stand 1 hour.
2. Heat vegetable oil in frying pan. Cook fish on both sides until golden brown.
3. Serve hot.

SERVES 4

Ikan Masak Molek

MALAYSIA

(Steamed Fish in Sauce)

- 2 pounds fish fillets (sole, red snapper, or sea bass)
- ¼ teaspoon white pepper
- 1 teaspoon salt
- 1 cup lemon grass, finely minced
- ¼ cup fresh ginger root, finely sliced
- ½ cup shallots, finely minced
- 2 fresh red chilies, minced
- 1 teaspoon lemon rind, grated
- 1 cup coconut milk
- 2 teaspoons parsley, chopped

1. Rub fish fillets with pepper and salt. Top with lemon grass. Steam until fish is cooked (about 25 minutes).
2. In saucepan bring to boil ginger root, shallots, chilies, lemon rind, and coconut milk. Mix well. Simmer for 20 minutes.
3. Transfer fish fillets to a serving platter, and pour hot sauce over fish.
4. Garnish with chopped parsley.

SERVES 4

Achar Ikan

MALAYSIA

(Spicy Fish)

- 6–8 fillets of red snapper (sea bass or grouper may be substituted)
- ½ teaspoon turmeric powder
- 2 teaspoons salt
- 1 cup vegetable oil for frying
- 6 green chilies, thinly sliced
- ¾ cup shallots, sliced
- 2 cucumbers, cut lengthwise in quarters, sliced thinly
- ¼ cup fresh ginger root, thinly sliced
- 1 tablespoon garlic, finely minced
- ½ cup cider vinegar
- 2 tablespoons sugar

1. Rub fish fillets with salt and half the turmeric powder. Refrigerate 2 hours.
2. Heat oil in deep frying pan. Fry fish fillets. Drain and set aside.
3. Pour away most of the oil and sauté chilies, shallots, cucumber, ginger root, and garlic for 2 minutes.
4. Add remaining turmeric powder, vinegar, and sugar into mixture. Simmer for 6 minutes.
5. Place fish fillets on a large platter. Pour sauce on top and serve.

SERVES 4

Clams Rempah

SINGAPORE

(Clams in Spicy Sauce)

- 2 tablespoons vegetable oil
- 1 cup shallots, finely minced
- 2 tablespoons fresh ginger root, finely minced
- 2 green chilies, finely chopped
- 1 tablespoon garlic, finely minced
- ¼ cup tomato sauce
- 2¼ cups fish stock
- 1 teaspoon sugar
- ¼ teaspoon salt
- ⅛ teaspoon black pepper, freshly ground
- 1 pound little neck clams, scrubbed and cleaned
- 2 teaspoons cornstarch
- water

1. Heat oil in large saucepan. Stir-fry shallots, ginger, chilies, and garlic 5 minutes.
2. Add tomato sauce, fish stock, sugar, salt, and pepper.
3. Combine cornstarch and a little water. Add to sauce.
4. Bring to a boil, stirring frequently. Add clams. Reduce heat and simmer about 5 minutes or until clams open.
5. Serve hot.

SERVES 4

T'ang Tsu Ming Hsia

CHINA

(Sweet and Sour Prawns)

- 12 prawns (or 24 medium shrimps, shelled and deveined)
- ¼ teaspoon salt
- ¼ teaspoon black pepper, freshly ground
- 5 teaspoons cornstarch
- 2 cups vegetable oil
- 3 tablespoons vinegar
- 3 tablespoons soy sauce
- 1½ tablespoons dry sherry
- 1½ tablespoons sugar
- ⅓ teaspoon salt
- 1 cucumber, sliced

1. Sprinkle prawns with salt and pepper. Coat with 2 teaspoons cornstarch.
2. Heat oil in frying pan over high heat. Fry prawns 2 minutes. Drain and set aside.
3. Remove oil from pan except for 3 tablespoons. Sauté the remaining ingredients except cucumber slices until mixture thickens. Return prawns to pan and mix well.
4. Transfer to serving platter. Garnish with cucumber slices.

Serves 6

Gwoo Lo Yue Lau

CHINA

(Sweet-Sour Fish)

- 1 2–3 pound red snapper (or sea bass or grouper), cleaned and scaled
- 1 egg, beaten
- ¼ cup cornstarch
- 3–4 cups vegetable oil

1. Make diagonal slashes on each side of fish. Dip fish in beaten egg, then dredge well with cornstarch.
2. Heat oil in frying pan. Fry fish 5 to 6 minutes each side.
3. Drain on paper towel. Transfer to serving dish. Pour sauce on top.

Sauce:

- 3 tablespoons vegetable oil
- 1 cup onion, finely minced
- 3 tablespoons fresh ginger root, finely minced
- 2 teaspoons garlic, finely minced
- 1 cup sugar
- 2 tablespoons cornstarch
- 4 tablespoons soy sauce
- 2 cups wine vinegar
- 3 tablespoons tomato sauce
- 1 tablespoon dry sherry

1. Heat oil in sauce pan. Sauté garlic, ginger, and onion until onion is transparent.
2. Add other ingredients, stirring until mixture thickens.
3. Pour on top of fish.

SERVES 4

Hoi Seen Jeung Boon Yue Lau

CHINA

(Fish Fillets with Hoi Sin Sauce)

- 1 teaspoon garlic, finely minced
- 1 tablespoon soy sauce
- 1 teaspoon fresh finger, finely grated
- 1½ teaspoons *hoi sin* sauce
- 1 pound fish fillets, cleaned and skinned (any firm, white-meat fish may be used)
- 3 tablespoons vegetable oil
- ½ cup scallions, finely minced

1. In a bowl, mix thoroughly garlic, soy sauce, ginger, and *hoi sin* sauce. Set aside.
2. Heat oil in frying pan or wok. Fry fish fillets, turning frequently.
3. Add garlic, ginger, soy sauce, and *hoi sin* mixture. Cover. Simmer 3 minutes.
4. Transfer to a serving dish. Garnish with scallions.

SERVES 4

Ca Hap

VIETNAM

(Steamed Trout)

- 1 whole trout or sea bass (1–1½ pounds)
- 1 tablespoon ginger root, shredded
- 1 teaspoon sugar
- 5 shallots, finely minced
- ½ cup pork shoulder with a little fat, finely sliced
- 5 tablespoons fish sauce
- 5 dried mushrooms, soaked in warm water till tender, cut julienne style
- 2 tablespoons fresh coriander, minced
- ½ teaspoon black pepper, freshly ground

1. Clean fish. Make diagonal slashes on both sides.
2. In an oven-proof bowl (large enough to hold the fish), mix all ingredients together. Coat fish with mixture. Let stand 1 hour.
3. Steam fish over boiling water 45 minutes or until the fish is done.
4. Serve hot.

SERVES 2

Pazoon Kyaw

BURMA

(Fried Prawns)

- 1 teaspoon ground turmeric
- 1 teaspoon salt
- 1 teaspoon chili powder
- 12 prawns, peeled and deveined
- 2 tablespoons peanut oil
- 2 tablespoons sesame oil

1. Combine turmeric, salt, and chili powder. Mix with prawns.
2. Combine peanut and sesame oils in large skillet. Heat over medium high heat.
3. Fry prawns until done (about 6 minutes).

SERVES 4

Nga Santan

BURMA

(Fish in Coconut Cream)

- 2 pounds whitefish or bluefish fillets, cut in 1-inch squares
- 1 teaspoon dried chili pepper
- 1 cup onion, finely minced
- 1 teaspoon ginger powder
- 1 tablespoon garlic, finely minced
- 1 tablespoon cornstarch
- 1 teaspoon salt
- 2 tablespoons lemon juice
- ½ teaspoon turmeric
- ½ cup vegetable oil
- 1 medium onion, peeled and sliced
- 1 cup coconut cream

1. In food processor, combine fish, chili pepper, minced onion, ginger, and garlic. Process until finely ground.
2. Transfer to mixing bowl. Add cornstarch, salt, lemon juice, and turmeric. Mix well and shape into small balls.
3. Heat oil in skillet. Sauté sliced onion until transparent. Remove onion and set aside. In same skillet fry fish balls until brown. Remove and drain on paper towels.
4. In same skillet, add coconut cream and simmer gently about 10 minutes.
5. Add fish balls and simmer over low heat an additional 10 minutes.
6. Serve on a platter. Garnish with sautéed onions.

SERVES 4

Nga Kyaw

BURMA

(Hot Fried Fish)

- 2–3 pounds catfish, cleaned and cut in 2-inch pieces
- ⅓ teaspoon turmeric
- 2 tablespoons fish sauce
- ½ cup vegetable oil
- 2 cups onions, minced
- 1 teaspoon tamarind paste (or 2 tablespoons lime juice) mixed with 1 cup water
- 2 teaspoons chili powder
- ¾ teaspoon shrimp paste
- 10 scallions, cut in 3-inch pieces

1. Rub turmeric and fish sauce on catfish pieces. Set aside.
2. Heat oil in skillet. Sauté onions until transparent. Remove and drain. Set aside and reserve for garnish.
3. Fry fish until done. Remove and drain.
4. Stir tamarind paste and water together to make tamarind juice.
5. Add chili powder to skillet. Heat, then add tamarind or lime mixture. Add shrimp paste and stir well for 8 minutes.
6. Add fish. Simmer, uncovered, until sauce is reduced. Turn fish to avoid sticking.
7. Add scallions, cover, and cook 3 minutes longer.
8. Serve on a platter, pouring sauce over fish. Garnish with reserved onions.

SERVES 4

Nga See Byan

BURMA

(Fish Curry)

- 2½–3 pounds codfish, cut in 2-inch pieces
- 1½ teaspoons salt
- ⅔ cup vegetable oil
- ½ teaspoon turmeric
- 3 cloves garlic, finely minced
- 2 cups onions, finely chopped
- 1 teaspoon ginger powder
- 1 teaspoon chili powder
- 2 cups tomatoes, chopped
- 1 tablespoon fish sauce
- ½ cup water
- ¾ cup scallions, minced

1. Mix fish with salt and turmeric. Set aside.
2. Heat oil in skillet. Fry fish about 4 minutes on each side. Drain and set aside.
3. In same skillet, sauté garlic and onion until transparent. Add ginger and chili powder. Stir well.
4. Add tomatoes and fish sauce. Cook 3 minutes longer.
5. Return fish to skillet and add water. Cover and simmer 15 minutes.
6. Add scallions before serving.

SERVES 4

Teriyaki

JAPAN

(Glazed Fish)

2 pounds salmon fillets (sea bass, mackerel, or tuna may be substituted)

Sauce:

1 cup soy sauce

½ cup sugar

1 cup sake or sherry

1. Mix sauce ingredients thoroughly. Add fish fillets and marinate 1 hour.
2. Drain. Place fish in pre-heated broiler. Cook 5 minutes on each side. Baste occasionally with sauce.
3. When done, remove from broiler. Pour remaining sauce over fish.
4. Serve hot.

Serves 6

Tempura

JAPAN

(Batter-Fried Shrimp and Vegetables)

1 cup water

1 egg

1 cup all-purpose flour

1 cup vegetable oil

24 large raw shrimps, shelled and deveined

½ pound string beans

1 green bell pepper, cut into julienne strips

3 carrots, cut into julienne strips

1 eggplant, cut into julienne strips

1 medium zucchini, cut into julienne strips

1. In a mixing bowl, combine water and egg. Beat lightly. Add flour gradually until blended. Mixture will be lumpy.
2. Pour oil into a deep frying pan. Heat to 350°F.
3. Dip shrimps, beans, pepper, carrots, eggplant, and zucchini, one slice at a time, into the batter. Fry in the oil, a few pieces at a time, until golden brown. Drain on paper towels.
4. Serve hot with sauce.

Sauce:

- ¾ cup *dashi* (see glossary)
- ¼ cup soy sauce
- ¼ cup sake
- 2 teaspoons sugar
- 4 tablespoons grated *daikon* (white Japanese radish)
- 1 tablespoon horseradish, grated
- 1 teaspoon ginger root, grated

1. Combine *dashi*, soy sauce, sake, and sugar. Mix well. Use this as the sauce.
2. In separate bowls, place the *daikon*, horseradish, and ginger root, and use as accompaniments.

SERVES 4–6

Pa Khing

LAOS and CAMBODIA

(Steamed Fish with Young Ginger)

- ⅔ cup lemon juice
- ½ cup ginger root, finely minced
- 3 tablespoons vegetable oil
- 2 tablespoons sesame oil
- 3 tablespoons garlic, finely minced
- 3 tablespoons sesame seeds
- 3 tablespoons soy sauce
- 2 pounds fish fillets (sole, red snapper, or sea bass)
- banana leaves or aluminum foil

1. Combine lemon juice and minced ginger root. Set aside.
2. Combine vegetable and sesame oils in a frying pan and heat. Add garlic and sauté until light brown. Remove garlic from oil and mix into lemon juice and ginger root mixture.
3. Fry sesame seeds in same pan until golden brown. Add to ginger mixture. Blend in soy sauce.
4. Sprinkle mixture over fish fillets. Steam in individual banana leaves or aluminum foil packages for 20 minutes.

SERVES 4

Koy Pa

LAOS and CAMBODIA

(Raw Fish Salad)

- 1 pound whitefish fillets, finely chopped
- ½ cup lemon juice
- 1 fresh chili, seeded and thinly sliced
- 2 teaspoons garlic, finely minced
- ½ cup scallions, finely minced
- 8 raw green beans, thinly sliced
- 1 tablespoon fish sauce
- lettuce leaves
- coriander leaves
- mint leaves

1. Marinate chopped fish fillets in lemon juice. Place in refrigerator overnight.
2. When ready to serve, combine fish fillets with chili, garlic, scallions, green beans, and fish sauce.
3. To serve, divide mixture into 6 portions and place each portion in the center of a lettuce leaf. Garnish with coriander and mint leaves.

SERVES 6

Ikan Panggang

INDONESIA

(Baked Fish)

2 pounds grouper or red snapper fillets (sea bass or bluefish may be substituted)

3 teaspoons lemon juice

2 teaspoons salt

1 tablespoon dried red hot chili, soaked in hot water for 10 minutes

½ teaspoon turmeric

4 tablespoons coconut milk

½ cup onion, finely minced

½ cup red tomatoes, chopped

aluminum foil

1. Brush fish with lemon juice and salt. Set aside for 20 minutes.
2. In a food processor, process the chili, turmeric, coconut milk, onion, and tomatoes to a smooth paste.
3. Place fish fillets on a large piece of aluminum foil and spread one-third of the paste on top of the fish. Broil fish on one side 2 minutes.
4. Turn fish over and spread with another third of the paste. Broil 2 minutes.
5. Return fillets to the first side, spread with remaining paste, and broil 2 minutes longer.
6. Serve hot.

SERVES 6

Satay Panggang Udang Brebes

INDONESIA

(Marinated Shrimp Barbecue)

1 pound fresh shrimp, peeled, deveined

12 bamboo skewers

Marinade:

2 tablespoons garlic, finely minced

1 tablespoon fresh lemon juice

1 teaspoon sugar

1 teaspoon salt

2 tablespoons water

½ teaspoon shrimp paste

3 fresh red or green semi-hot chilies, minced

¼ cup sweet pepper, finely sliced

1. In large mixing bowl, combine all marinade ingredients. Mix well to form a smooth paste.
2. Marinate shrimp 2 hours. Place 4 shrimps on each skewer, and broil over charcoal or in a gas broiler 5 minutes.
3. Baste occasionally during broiling with the marinade.

Serves 4

Escabeche

THE PHILIPPINES

(Sweet-and-Sour Fish)

2 pounds whole red snapper (sea bass, bluefish, or carp may be substituted)

salt to taste

1 cup white vinegar

1 cup water

½ cup sugar

4 tablespoons vegetable oil

2 cups diced bean curd

6 tablespoons garlic, minced

1 cup onion, chopped

4 tablespoons ginger, sliced julienne-style

2 cups mushrooms, sliced

1 cup bell pepper, cut in strips

1 tablespoon sifted flour

1. Clean fish and slit open. Season with salt inside and out.
2. Mix vinegar, water, sugar, and salt for sweet-sour taste. Set aside.
3. Heat oil in a skillet. Fry fish and bean curd. Remove both from pan and set aside.
3. In same skillet, sauté garlic until light brown, then onion until transparent. Add ginger and the vinegar mixture. Bring mixture to a boil.
5. Add fried fish, bean curd pieces, mushrooms, and pepper. Add flour to thicken. Stir lightly. Cover the skillet and simmer 5 minutes.
6. Serve hot.

SERVES 4

Fish Sarciado

THE PHILIPPINES

(Fish with Tomato Sauce)

1 pound fish fillets (sole, red snapper, or sea bass)

1 teaspoon salt

1 tablespoon lemon juice

½ cup vegetable or corn oil

2 tablespoons garlic, minced

¼ cup onion, minced

1 cup tomatoes, minced

½ teaspoon pepper, freshly ground

¼ cup water

1 teaspoon fish sauce or salt

¼ cup scallions, chopped

1. Season fish with salt and lemon juice. Let stand for 20 minutes.
2. In large skillet, using half the oil, fry fillets until light brown on both sides. Drain on paper towel.
3. In another large skillet, sauté garlic in remaining oil until light brown, then onion until transparent. Add tomatoes and cook until soft. Add pepper, water, and fish sauce or salt. Simmer until slightly thickened.
4. Add fried fish to sauce. Cover skillet and cook 2 minutes, turning fillets once.
5. Serve hot, garnished with scallions.

SERVES 4

Fish Tinola

THE PHILIPPINES

(Boiled Fish)

1 tablespoon vegetable or corn oil

1 cup onion, chopped

1 tablespoon garlic, finely minced

1 tablespoon ginger, finely minced

2 cups water

1 pound whole fish (snapper or other firm, white-meat fish)

2 cups sliced zucchini

fish sauce or salt to taste

½ teaspoon pepper, freshly ground

1. Heat oil in saucepan. Sauté onion, garlic, and ginger, until onion is transparent. Add water and bring to a boil.
2. Add fish and zucchini. Season with fish sauce or salt and pepper. Simmer until done.
3. Serve hot.

SERVES 2

Pork

The earliest Asian recipes for pork come from China, where a small, wild species was domesticated about 3000 B.C., about 1,500 years before Europeans domesticated the indigenous wild boar. A Chinese recipe dating from 500 B.C. describes roasting a suckling pig in an oven buried in the earth. The pig was stuffed with dates and covered with straw mixed with clay. This ancient recipe is followed today in Polynesia, where pig meat is celebrated as a marvel of the table.

Pork is the main animal meat eaten in Asia, and China is the world's leading pork-eating nation. This accounts for the tremendous number of pork recipes in Chinese cuisine.

Despite the restrictions of Islam, which is the dominant religion in Malaysia, Indonesia, and parts of the Philippines and Singapore, Asians consider pork a truly versatile source of protein. It is economical to raise and has virtually no wasted parts. A versatile ingredient in all types of preparations, pork dishes rival those based on fish at banquets and everyday meals as well.

Generally, dishes made from pork are bathed in sweet and sour sauces made from soy sauce, ginger, and honey or sugar. In Indochina, especially in Vietnam, a superior pork is obtained from pigs fed on chopped banana trunks. Vietnamese cooks consider this type of pork more tender and more deliciously flavored than other less carefully fed animals. In Laos, the national dish is made of fresh pork skin sliced into strips and roasted with mushrooms, string beans, and eggplant. The national dish of the Philippines is *lechon*, suckling pig roasted whole over live coals and served with a traditional sauce made of liver and pickled papaya fruit, called *achara*.

The recipes in this section demonstrate the versatility of pork and the many combinations that can be obtained with vegetables, seafood, noodles, and various sauces.

Wetha Seen Byan

BURMA

(Full Flavor Pork)

- 3 pounds boneless pork (shoulder or butt), cut in 2-inch cubes
- 1½ teaspoons salt
- 1½ cups onion, finely minced
- 2 teaspoons ginger powder
- 2 teaspoons chili powder
- ⅓ teaspoon turmeric
- 1 tablespoon fish sauce
- 1 teaspoon shrimp paste
- 1 tablespoon soy sauce
- ½ cup vegetable oil
- water
- 1 tablespoon cider vinegar
- 1 head garlic, finely minced

1. In large pot combine pork, salt, onions, ginger powder, chili powder, turmeric, fish sauce, shrimp paste, soy sauce, and oil. Mix well. Cover with water and bring to a boil.
2. Simmer until meat is tender (about 45 minutes).
3. Add vinegar and finely minced garlic. Simmer 15 minutes longer.
4. Serve hot.

SERVES 6

Wetha Seen

BURMA

(Middle Country Pork Packets)

Banana leaves were originally used in this recipe, a favorite of traders who cross the area called Middle Country—the area between the Shan Hills and the great plains of the heart of Burma.

- 3 pounds boneless pork shoulder or butt, finely ground
- 20 8-inch squares aluminum foil (or banana leaves)
- ⅓ teaspoon turmeric
- 1 teaspoon salt
- 3 teaspoons garlic, finely minced
- 1 onion, chopped
- 1 cup flour
- 1 cup chives, finely minced
- 5 tablespoons vegetable oil
- 1½ tablespoons soy sauce

1. Combine ground pork with turmeric, salt, garlic, onion, flour, chives, oil, and soy sauce. Mix well.
2. Mound one heaping tablespoon of pork mixture in center of foil and fold foil into a triangle by joining opposite corners together. Press sides to seal. Repeat with remaining mixture, until all pork has been used.
3. Place on a rack in a steamer and steam 30 minutes.
4. Serve with sauce.

Sauce:

3 tablespoons vegetable oil

3 tablespoons garlic, finely minced

½ tablespoon ginger powder

½ teaspoon chili powder

3 tablespoons cider vinegar

½ teaspoon sugar

Salt to taste

1. Sauté garlic in oil until golden. Add ginger powder, chili powder, vinegar, sugar, and salt.
2. Mix and simmer 3 minutes.
3. Spoon onto opened pork packets.

Serves 6

Cha Dum

VIETNAM

(Meat Loaf)

1 package bean noodles

water

1 pound pork, ground

1 teaspoon salt

1 teaspoon black pepper, freshly ground

4 cloves garlic, finely minced

3 shallots, finely minced

1 teaspoon fish sauce or soy sauce

5 eggs, slightly beaten

1. Boil water. Soak bean noodles in hot water 30 minutes. Drain. Chop into 1-inch pieces. Set aside 1 cup of noodles and reserve balance for other uses.
2. In large mixing bowl, combine pork, salt, pepper, garlic, shallots, fish sauce, and bean noodles.
3. Add eggs to mixture. Shape into meat loaf and place in ovenproof container.
4. Place ovenproof container in larger pan. Add water to the base of the pan and bake until done (about 20 minutes).

SERVES 4–6

Thit Kho Nuoc Dua

VIETNAM

(Pork with Coconut Milk)

1 pound pork shoulder, with some fat, cut in 1½-inch cubes

¼ teaspoon black pepper, freshly ground

3 shallots, finely minced

3 tablespoons fish sauce

2 cups coconut milk

1. Marinate pork in a mixture of pepper, shallots, and fish sauce overnight in refrigerator.
2. In large saucepan simmer coconut milk about 8 minutes until light brown. Add meat to coconut milk. Simmer about 2 hours.
3. Add water if liquid becomes sticky. Stir occasionally throughout cooking time.

SERVES 4–6

Jang

THAILAND

(Roast Pork)

1 pound pork chops

3/4 teaspoon black pepper, freshly ground

1 tablespoon coriander root, finely chopped

4 teaspoon garlic, finely minced

1 tablespoon fish sauce

5 teaspoons soy sauce

1. Marinate pork chops in pepper, coriander, garlic, fish sauce, and soy sauce. Place in refrigerator over night.
2. Roast marinated pork chops in oven or grill over charcoal fire.
3. Serve hot.

SERVES 4

T'ang Tsu Chu Jo

CHINA

(Spareribs with Sweet-Sour Sauce)

- 1 cup water
- 1 pound pork spareribs, cut in 2-inch pieces
- 3 tablespoons cornstarch
- 2 teaspoons soy sauce
- 2 cups vegetable oil
- 1 cup onion, finely sliced
- ½ cup water
- 1 cup vinegar
- ¾ cup sugar
- ¼ cup soy sauce

1. Boil spareribs in water 30 minutes. Drain.
2. Dip spareribs in 1 tablespoon cornstarch and 2 teaspoons soy sauce.
3. Heat oil in frying pan. Fry spareribs until brown. Set spareribs aside.
4. Sauté onion. Set aside.
5. Combine water, vinegar, sugar, remaining cornstarch, and soy sauce in saucepan. Simmer 5 minutes.
6. Add spareribs and onions to sauce and simmer 5 minutes longer.
7. Serve hot.

SERVES 4

Asadong Baboy

THE PHILIPPINES

(Pork Chinese-Style)

2 pounds pork loin

Marinade:

1 cup water

⅓ cup soy sauce

⅓ cup brown sugar

2 tablespoons white wine

½ teaspoon salt

2 tablespoons finely minced garlic

1. Combine all marinade ingredients in a large pot. Mix well.
2. Marinate the whole pork loin 30 minutes or more in the pot.
3. Cover pot and bring mixture to a boil.
4. Lower heat and simmer until meat is tender (about 30 minutes).
5. Serve hot with marinade.

SERVES 6

Pork Estofado

THE PHILIPPINES

(Pork Braised with Sugar)

- ¼ cup vegetable or corn oil
- 4 tablespoons minced garlic
- 1 pound lean pork, cut into cubes
- ½ cup apple cider vinegar
- ¼ cup soy sauce
- ⅓ cup sugar
- ½ cup water
- 1 bay leaf
- 8 peppercorns, crushed
- 1 carrot, cut into 1-inch strips
- 2 plantains, cut ½-inch thick diagonally and fried in oil
- 2 pieces French bread, cut into 1-inch cubes and fried in oil

1. In a skillet, heat oil and brown garlic.
2. Add pork cubes and fry until brown.
3. Add vinegar, soy sauce, sugar, water, bay leaf, and peppercorns. Bring to a boil without stirring. Lower flame and cook until the pork is almost done.
4. Add carrot. Continue cooking until the pork is tender.
5. Before serving, garnish with fried plantains and French bread cubes.

SERVES 4

Almondigas

THE PHILIPPINES

(Pork with Vermicelli)

1 egg

1 pound ground pork

1 tablespoon celery, chopped

2 tablespoons onion, chopped

1 teaspoon garlic powder (or 2 cloves garlic, minced)

1 teaspoon salt

⅛ teaspoon pepper

3 cups water

1 bundle vermicelli or *misua*

1. Beat egg. Add pork, celery, onion, garlic, salt, and pepper. Mix well.
2. Shape mixture into 1-inch balls.
3. Bring 3 cups water to a boil. Add pork balls and vermicelli (or *misua*) and simmer another 5 minutes, or until done. Serve hot.

SERVES 4

Chu Ju Chin Jow

CHINA

(Pork with Peppers and Cashews)

1½ pounds pork tenderloin, cut in ¾-inch cubes

½ teaspoon sugar

2½ tablespoons soy sauce

1 tablespoon cornstarch

½ cup chicken stock (or water)

3 tablespoons vegetable oil

1 onion, cut into ¾-inch cubes

1 red bell pepper, cut into ¾-inch cubes

1 green bell pepper, cut into ¾-inch cubes

2 tablespoons soy sauce

½ cup cashew nuts

1. Marinate pork tenderloin cubes in sugar and soy sauce 1 hour.
2. Mix cornstarch and chicken stock (or water).
3. In frying pan or wok, heat 3 tablespoons oil. Stir-fry pork 5 minutes. Add vegetables and stir-fry 3 minutes more.
4. Add soy sauce and liquified cornstarch. Continue stirring until sauce thickens.
5. Add the cashew nuts. Simmer, stirring continuously, 2 minutes more.
6. Serve immediately.

SERVES 4

T'ang Tsu Pai Gu

CHINA

(Sweet and Sour Pork)

- ¼ teaspoon Chinese Five Spice powder
- ½ teaspoon ground black pepper
- ½ teaspoon salt
- 1 pound pork tenderloin, cut into 1 inch cubes
- 2 eggs
- 1 tablespoon Chinese wine
- 1 tablespoon soy sauce
- 2 ounces cornstarch
- 2 cups vegetable oil

1. Mix Five Spice powder, pepper, and salt with the pork cubes.
2. Beat eggs, add wine and soy sauce. Combine pork with this mixture. Marinate one hour. Remove, coat with cornstarch.
3. Heat oil in frying pan. Cook meat until golden. Drain, set aside.

Sauce:

- 1 cup onion, chopped
- 1 cup green bell pepper, chopped
- 2 cups ripe tomato, chopped
- 2 cups cucumber, peeled and sliced
- 2 cups carrots, peeled and sliced
- 2 fresh red chilies, cut julienne style
- ½ cup fresh ginger root, cut julienne style
- 1 teaspoon garlic, finely minced
- 1 cup chicken stock
- 1 tablespoon Chinese wine
- 1 tablespoon soy sauce
- 1 tablespoon cider vinegar
- 1 tablespoon fresh lemon juice
- 4 tablespoons tomato sauce
- 4 tablespoons sugar
- 1 8-ounce can pineapple chunks
- cold water
- 2 teaspoons cornstarch

1. In same pan used for frying meat, stir-fry onion, bell pepper, tomato, cucumber, carrots, chili, ginger, and garlic 5 minutes.
2. Add chicken stock, wine, soy sauce, vinegar, lemon juice, tomato sauce, sugar, and pineapple chunks. Stir and blend thoroughly. Simmer over low heat 3 minutes.
3. Mix cornstarch and small quantity cold water. Add to vegetable mixture in frying pan.
4. Add pork. Stir-fry 2 minutes.
5. Serve hot on large platter.

SERVES 4

Chu Ju Szu Ch'ao Chu Sun

CHINA

(Pork with Bamboo Shoots)

- 6 tablespoons vegetable oil
- 2 cups canned bamboo shoots, sliced lengthwise
- 2 tablespoons soy sauce
- ½ teaspoon salt
- 1 tablespoon cornstarch
- 2 tablespoons dry sherry
- 1 pound pork tenderloin, cut into fine slices
- ½ cup water

1. Heat 4 tablespoons vegetable oil in frying pan. Sauté bamboo shoots 4 minutes. Remove from pan and drain.
2. Mix soy sauce, salt, cornstarch, and sherry. Dredge pork until coated.
3. Reheat pan, adding 2 tablespoons vegetable oil. Fry pork slices until tender (about 8 minutes).
4. Add sautéed bamboo shoots and ½ cup of water. Simmer over moderate heat 5 minutes longer.
5. Serve hot.

SERVES 4

Babi Goreng Meehoon

MALAYSIA

(Fried Pork with Vermicelli)

- ¼ pound *meehoon* (fine rice vermicelli)
- warm water for soaking
- 3 tablespoons vegetable oil
- 1 cup potato, cubed
- 2 cups onion, finely sliced
- 1 tablespoon garlic, finely minced
- ½ pound pork belly, fat and skin removed, diced
- 3 tablespoons soy sauce
- ½ cup water
- ⅛ teaspoon ground black pepper
- 3 teaspoons sugar

1. Soak *meehoon* in warm water 5 minutes. Drain and set aside.
2. Heat oil in large frying pan and sauté potato until golden brown. Drain and set aside.
3. Sauté onions and garlic 3 minutes. Add diced pork belly. Stir until pork is cooked and golden brown.
4. Add *meehoon*, soy sauce, and water. Continue stirring for 3 minutes longer.
5. Add pepper and sugar. Continue stirring until liquid is almost absorbed.
6. Stir in potatoes. Serve hot.

SERVES 4

Babi Satay

MALAYSIA

(Skewered Pork)

2 tablespoons vegetable oil

1 strip lemon rind

1½ cup onion, finely minced

1 tablespoon soy sauce

2 tablespoons roasted peanuts

2 teaspoons ground coriander

1 teaspoon sugar

1 teaspoon salt

1 teaspoon ground cumin

1 teaspoon ground turmeric

¼ teaspoon ground cinnamon

1 pound pork fillet, cut in 1-inch cubes

bamboo skewers

1. In food processor, mix oil, lemon rind, onion, soy sauce, peanuts, coriander, sugar, salt, cumin, turmeric, and cinnamon. Blend until smooth.
2. Marinate cubed pork fillets in mixture overnight.
3. Thread on bamboo skewers. Grill over charcoal (or broil).
4. Serve hot.

SERVES 4

Galbi Jim

KOREA

(Spareribs with Sesame Sauce)

- 2 tablespoons vegetable oil
- 3 pounds pork spareribs, cut in 2-inch cubes
- 2 tablespoons toasted, ground sesame seeds
- 2 tablespoons sherry
- 1 tablespoon garlic, finely minced
- ½ cup scallions, finely minced
- 2 tablespoons soy sauce
- 3 teaspoons sesame oil
- 2½ tablespoons sugar
- 1 teaspoon fresh ginger, finely grated
- 1 cup water
- 2 teaspoons cornstarch
- 2 teaspoons cold water

1. In large saucepan, heat oil. Brown spareribs. Add sesame seeds, sherry, garlic, scallions, soy sauce, sesame oil, sugar, ginger, and water. Mix well. Bring to boil.
2. Cover and simmer one hour over low heat.
3. Mix cornstarch and water in a bowl, until mixture is a paste-like consistency. Pour into saucepan.
4. Mix well and serve hot.

SERVES 6

Babi Ketjap

INDONESIA

(Pork in Soy Sauce)

3 pounds pork tenderloin, cut into 1-inch cubes

3 tablespoons vegetable oil

½ cup *ketjap* (Indonesian soy sauce)

6 slices fresh ginger root

6 garlic cloves

1½ teaspoons brown sugar

1 teaspoon salt

water

1. In large frying pan, brown pork tenderloin cubes in oil. Set aside.
2. Blend *ketjap*, ginger root, garlic, brown sugar, and salt in food processor until smooth.
3. Add this mixture to meat. Add enough water to cover pork. Simmer over low heat until pork is tender, about 30 minutes.
4. Serve hot.

SERVES 4

Buta Teriyaki

JAPAN

(Grilled Marinated Pork)

- 2 pounds pork loin, thinly sliced
- ⅓ cup soy sauce
- ¼ cup sugar
- 1 teaspoon fresh ginger root, grated
- 1 cup onion, finely minced
- ¼ cup sake

1. Combine pork slices, soy sauce, sugar, ginger root, onion, and sake. Marinate overnight in refrigerator.
2. Thread pork onto skewers. Broil or grill 5 minutes on each side while basting frequently with the marinade.
3. Serve hot.

SERVES 4

Beef

Beef may the "the soul of cooking" in the West (as the great nineteenth-century French chef Marie-Antoine Carême put it), but in Asia it is a relatively new ingredient. Beef is an uneconomical food to raise, requiring vast pasturage areas which are not readily available in this densely populated part of the world. Abhorred as a food source by Buddhist tradition, the eating of beef began in Asia only after its introduction by the European explorers of the fifteenth and sixteenth centuries. At the time, Asians despised these eaters of red meat for their "disagreeable" body odor.

In most of Asia, even today, cattle is generally considered too precious a beast of burden to be slaughtered and eaten, and therefore there are relatively few beef dishes in the cuisines of these countries. This is not true in Japan, where the cooking and eating of beef is traditionally dated to the 1850s, when a cow was butchered for the table of an American consul. The event was immortalized by the raising of a monument by Japan's butchers' association. The Emperor of Japan first ate beef in 1872. Today, Kobe beef, considered the world's best, comes from Japan. Steers of Kobe are hand-fed on Kirin beer, massaged daily, and given individual care. The result is an astronomically expensive beef that is incredibly tender, exquisitely flavored, and richly marbled. It is not an everyday dish.

The Spanish colonization of the Philippines influenced the cuisine of that nation heavily, and it is there, more than anywhere else in Asia, that the eating of beef and veal is relatively common. Later American influence refined Filipino beef cookery.

Throughout the rest of Asia, beef is the aristocrat of modern cuisine. From Kobe or elsewhere, it is an expensive meat, and its appearance on the table signals a celebration or a feast.

For Asians, as one Japanese historian has remarked, "to eat beef is a sign of an advanced state of civilization."

A Meta Pyuk

BURMA

(Beef Stew or Simmered Beef)

- 3 pounds stewing beef, cut in 2-inch cubes
- 1½ tablespoons cider vinegar
- ⅓ teaspoon turmeric
- 2 tablespoons fish sauce
- 4 teaspoons garlic, finely minced
- 1 teaspoon chili powder
- 1½ cups onion, finely minced
- 2 teaspoons ginger powder
- ½ cup vegetable oil
- water
- 1 teaspoon salt
- 3 bay leaves
- 2 cinnamon sticks
- 5 cloves, whole
- 10 black peppercorns

1. Marinate beef in mixture of vinegar, turmeric, and fish sauce overnight.
2. In large pan, mix meat with garlic, chili powder, onion, ginger powder, and vegetable oil. Add enough water to cover. Bring to a boil.
3. Lower heat and simmer 30 minutes. Add more water if needed. Continue simmering until tender, stirring mixture occasionally.
4. Add salt, bay leaves, cinnamon, cloves, and peppercorns. Continue cooking until oil on top is clear.

SERVES 6

Bo Vien

VIETNAM

(Beef Balls)

- 2 pounds beef round, cut in thin, 2-inch square slices
- 6 tablespoons water
- 6 tablespoons fish sauce
- 1 tablespoon corn starch
- ½ teaspoon sugar
- 2 teaspoons baking powder
- ¼ teaspoon black pepper, freshly ground
- 3 tablespoons sesame oil
- 2 quarts water

1. Place meat in a mixing bowl and add 6 tablespoons water, fish sauce, corn starch, sugar, baking powder, and pepper. Marinate meat in mixture overnight.
2. In a food processor, puree the meat to a paste-like consistency.
3. Rub sesame oil in palm of hand; scoop 1 tablespoon of meat into palm and shape into a ball. Repeat with rest of meat.
4. Boil 2 quarts water. Drop in meatballs and boil 8 minutes. Remove from the water and drain. Reserve cooking water.

Stock:

Water reserved from boiling meatballs

½ teaspoon salt

3 teaspoons fish sauce

1. Combine water, salt, and fish sauce. Reheat when ready to serve. Add meatballs and heat 5 minutes.
2. In individual soup bowls, place 4–5 meatballs and add broth.

Accompaniments:

1 cup scallions, finely chopped

1 teaspoon black pepper

chili paste with garlic

1. Sprinkle scallions and black pepper over meatballs and broth in soup bowls.
2. Serve chili paste with garlic in a separate dish, to be added to taste.

SERVES 4–6

Bo Xao Gia

VIETNAM

(Beef with Sprouts)

- 1 pound beef flank steak, cut in slices 1½″ by 1″, ⅛″ thick
- ¼ teaspoon garlic, finely minced
- ¼ teaspoon black pepper, freshly ground
- 1 medium onion, sliced lengthwise
- 6 tablespoons fish sauce
- 4 tablespoons vegetable oil
- 3 garlic cloves, crushed
- 2 pounds bean sprouts
- fish sauce to taste
- pepper to taste

1. Marinate steak, minced garlic, pepper, onion, and 3 tablespoons fish sauce 1 hour.
2. In frying pan, heat 2 tablespoons oil and sauté crushed garlic cloves. Add beef and fry until brown. Remove and set aside.
3. Add remaining oil to frying pan and heat. Add bean sprouts and 3 tablespoons fish sauce. Stir-fry 3 minutes.
4. Return beef to pan and continue to stir-fry. Add fish sauce and pepper to taste.

SERVES 4–6

See Yo Ngau Yook

CHINA

(Red-Cooked Beef)

- 4 pounds beef shin
- 2 cups soy sauce
- 4 cups water
- ½ cup dry sherry
- 3 tablespoons fresh ginger root, finely minced
- 3 tablespoons sugar
- 2 tablespoons sesame oil
- 3 whole star anise
- 2 teaspoons garlic, finely minced

1. In large saucepan, combine all ingredients with beef.
2. Bring to boil.
3. Cover, and let simmer 3¼ hours. Turn beef several times during cooking.
4. When beef is tender, uncover and simmer another 20 minutes.
5. Slice and serve.

Serves 8

Ho Lan Dau Chow Ngau Yook

CHINA

(Beef with Snow Peas)

1 pound beef rump steak, shredded

½ teaspoon salt

3 tablespoons soy sauce

8 dried Chinese mushrooms, soaked in warm water and drained

4 tablespoons vegetable oil

1½ cups snow peas, stringed

½ cup scallions, chopped

½ teaspoon sugar

½ cup beef stock

1 tablespoon dry sherry

4 teaspoons cornstarch

1 tablespoon water

1. Combine shredded beef, salt, and soy sauce. Set aside to marinate 1 hour.
2. Trim stems from mushrooms and slice caps in thin strips. Set aside.
3. Heat 2 tablespoons vegetable oil in frying pan and stir-fry mushrooms and snow peas 3 minutes. Set aside.
4. Heat remaining vegetable oil in frying pan. Cook beef over high heat 8 minutes or until color changes. Add scallions, sugar, beef stock, and dry sherry. Stir 2 minutes while cooking. Add cornstarch blended with water.
5. Return mushrooms and snow peas and heat thoroughly.
6. Serve hot.

SERVES 4

Ching Chiao Niu Jou

CHINA

(Shredded Beef with Green Pepper and Onion)

1 pound beef rump steak, shredded

¼ teaspoon baking soda

1 teaspoon cornstarch

2 teaspoons vegetable oil

1 tablespoon dry sherry

1 tablespoon soy sauce

½ teaspoon sugar

6 tablespoons vegetable oil

½ teaspoon salt

1 cup onion, shredded

½ cup green bell peppers, shredded

⅛ teaspoon black pepper, freshly ground

1. In large mixing bowl, combine shredded beef, baking soda, cornstarch, vegetable oil, dry sherry, soy sauce, and sugar. Set aside 1 hour.
2. In frying pan, heat 3 tablespoons vegetable oil. Add salt. Sauté onion and bell peppers 3 minutes. Remove from pan and set aside.
3. Heat remaining vegetable oil in pan and add beef. Stir-fry 5 minutes. Add pepper, sautéed onion, and bell peppers. Mix well, stir-frying 2 minutes longer.
4. Serve hot.

SERVES 4

Satay Daging

MALAYSIA

(Malay Beef Satay)

2 pounds rump steak, cut in 1-inch cubes

Marinade:

2 teaspoons lemon rind, finely grated

2 teaspoons fennel, ground

5 tablespoons coconut milk

1½ tablespoons sugar

2 tablespoons salt

2 teaspoons ground turmeric

2 teaspoons ground cumin

bamboo skewers

water for soaking

1. In large bowl, combine all the marinade ingredients and mix well.
2. Add cubed steak and marinate overnight.
3. Thread five pieces of meat onto a skewer that has been soaked in water for a half-hour.
4. Grill over hot coals or in broiler.
5. Serve hot.

SERVES 4

Kare-Kare

THE PHILIPPINES

(Oxtail Stew in Peanut-Butter Sauce)

- 3 pounds oxtail, cut into serving pieces
- 6 cups water
- 2 tablespoons garlic, finely minced
- 1 cup onion, chopped
- 4 tablespoons oil
- ½ cup *anatto* water
- ½ cup raw rice, ground to a powder in food processor and roasted in a pan until brown
- 1 cup peanut butter
- 1 eggplant, cut into serving pieces
- 10 string beans, cut into 2-inch lengths
- 1 small cabbage, quartered
- salt and pepper to taste
- shrimp paste to taste

1. Boil oxtail in 6 cups water for 1 hour, or until tender. Remove meat and reserve stock.
2. In a large saucepan, sauté garlic and onion in oil.
3. Add *anatto* water and oxtail to saucepan and bring to a boil.
4. Stir in roasted rice powder and peanut butter. Add four cups reserved stock, eggplant, string beans, and cabbage. Mix well.
5. Bring mixture to a boil. Reduce heat and simmer 10 minutes. Season with salt and pepper to taste.
6. Serve with shrimp paste.

SERVES 6–8

Karne Con Kutsay

THE PHILIPPINES

(Beef with Leeks)

1 pound beef tenderloin, cut in 1½-inch cubes

1 egg white

1 tablespoon cornstarch

1 cup oil

3 tablespoons soy sauce

3 tablespoons water

1 red pepper, cut in strips

¼ cup *kutsay* (leeks) cut in strips

2 tablespoons sesame oil

1. Coat tenderloin cubes with egg white, then with cornstarch. Let stand 15 minutes.
2. Add oil to deep fryer, deep fry beef, and drain. Leave 3 tablespoons of oil in pan.
3. Add soy sauce, water, red pepper, leeks, and meat. Cook 2 minutes.
4. Add sesame oil before serving.

SERVES 4

Bistek

THE PHILIPPINES

(Steak, Philippine-Style)*

- 2 pounds sirloin steak, cut in ¼-inch slices
- 2 tablespoons lemon juice
- 3 tablespoons soy sauce
- ½ teaspoon pepper, freshly ground
- salt to taste
- 1 cup onion rings, thinly sliced
- ¼ cup cooking oil
- ½ cup water

1. Marinate meat in lemon juice, soy sauce, pepper, and salt 3 hours or more.
2. In skillet fry onion rings in oil until transparent. Transfer to a serving dish, leaving oil in skillet.
3. Add meat to skillet and cook over high heat until tender, stirring often. Transfer meat to a serving dish.
4. Add marinade and water to the skillet, simmer 10 minutes, and pour over meat and onion rings.

SERVES 4

---

*This recipe can also be used for pork chops, liver, or fish.

Karne Asada

THE PHILIPPINES

(Beef Stew)

2 pounds beef sirloin, cut in 3-inch cubes

2 tablespoons lemon juice

2 tablespoons soy sauce

1½ tablespoons cornstarch

¼ teaspoon Maggi sauce or soy sauce

fish sauce or salt to taste

freshly ground pepper to taste

2 large potatoes, sliced thin

2 large onions, sliced in rings

3 tablespoons oil

1. Marinate sirloin cubes in lemon juice, soy sauce, cornstarch, Maggi, fish sauce or salt, and pepper 30 minutes.
2. Over low flame, simmer marinade and sirloin 1 hour.
3. In skillet, fry separately potatoes and onion rings in oil.
4. Arrange beef on platter with potatoes and onion rings on top.

SERVES 4

Daging Lembu Kichap

MALAYSIA

(Spicy Beef)

- 1 tablespoon fresh ginger root, peeled and grated
- 4 fresh red chilies, seeded and sliced
- 1 cup onion, finely chopped
- ¼ cup shallots, chopped
- 2 teaspoons garlic, finely minced
- 3 tablespoons lime or lemon juice
- 1 teaspoon salt
- ⅛ teaspoon black pepper, freshly ground
- 4 tablespoons vegetable oil
- 2 pounds lean beef (rump steak or tenderloin), cut in bite-size pieces
- 3 bay leaves
- 4 tablespoons soy sauce
- 1½ cup beef stock

1. In a food processor, blend to a paste-like consistency ginger root, chilies, onion, shallots, garlic, lime juice, salt, and pepper.
2. In large frying pan, heat oil, and stir-fry vegetable paste, stirring constantly for 5 minutes. Add the beef and continue stirring another 5 minutes.
3. Add bay leaves, soy sauce, and beef stock. Bring to a boil until meat is done (about 15 minutes).
4. Serve hot.

SERVES 4

Bul Galbi

KOREA

(Barbecued Short Ribs of Beef)

- 4 pounds beef short ribs, cut in 2-inch cubes

Marinade:

- ½ cup water
- ½ cup scallions, finely minced
- 1 teaspoon fresh ginger, finely grated
- 1 tablespoon sugar
- 3 teaspoons garlic, finely minced
- ½ teaspoon ground black pepper
- 3 tablespoons toasted sesame seeds, crushed
- ¾ cup soy sauce

1. In large mixing bowl, combine the marinade ingredients and mix well. Add ribs. Marinate overnight.
2. Grill or broil the ribs until done. (The ribs may also be roasted in moderately hot [300°F] oven 1 hour.)

SERVES 4

Bul Kogi

KOREA

(Grilled Beef Slices)

2 pounds boneless 1- to 2-inch sirloin steak (flank or chuck may be substituted), sliced thinly across the grain in ¼-inch slices

Marinade:

- 2 tablespoons vegetable oil
- 2 tablespoons sugar
- ½ cup dark soy sauce
- 3 tablespoons sherry
- 3 tablespoons roasted whole sesame seeds
- 1½ tablespoons garlic, finely minced
- ½ cup scallions, finely minced
- ½ teaspoon salt
- ½ teaspoon ground black pepper

1. In large mixing bowl, combine marinade ingredients. Mix well. Add meat and marinate overnight.
2. Remove meat from marinade and pat dry. Charcoal grill or broil for 3 minutes.
3. Serve hot.

Serves 4

Oyijikai

KOREA

(Stir-Fried Beef and Cucumber)

- 8 ounces lean beef fillet, cut in paper-thin slices, 2 inches long, ½-inch wide
- 2 teaspoons sesame oil
- ¼ teaspoon cayenne pepper
- ½ teaspoon sugar
- ½ teaspoon salt
- 1 tablespoon soy sauce
- 3 teaspoons vegetable oil
- 2 large cucumbers, peeled, seeded, and cut crosswise in medium thin slices
- 3 tablespoons toasted sesame seeds, crushed

1. Place beef fillet in mixing bowl. Add sesame oil, cayenne pepper, sugar, salt, and soy sauce. Marinate ½ hour.
2. In large frying pan, heat vegetable oil. Add beef fillet and stir-fry 2 minutes. Add cucumber and continue stir-frying until cucumber is cooked but still crisp.
3. Transfer to a serving dish and garnish with sesame seeds. Serve hot.

SERVES 4

Satay

INDONESIA

(Beef Barbecue)

2 pounds flank steak, cut in ¼-inch strips

25 bamboo skewers

Marinade:

4 teaspoons ground chili powder

4 tablespoons vegetable oil

2 teaspoons turmeric powder

1 teaspoon fresh ginger, grated

1 tablespoon peanut butter

2 tablespoons garlic, finely minced

1 teaspoon brown sugar

1 cup onion, finely minced

½ teaspoon lemon rind, grated

¾ cup water

1 teaspoon salt

1. Combine marinade ingredients in large saucepan. Simmer over moderate heat 5 minutes, until marinade has a smooth consistency.
2. Add beef. Simmer 3 minutes, stirring constantly. Set aside and let cool.
3. Thread meat on skewers. Broil on grill 3 minutes each side while basting with remaining marinade.
4. Serve hot.

SERVES 6

Empal

INDONESIA

(Spicy Fried Beef)

1 pound boneless beef chuck

3 cups water

½ cup vegetable oil

Marinade:

1 tablespoon garlic, finely minced

2 teaspoons coriander

1 teaspoon salt

1 teaspoon sugar

1 teaspoon tamarind paste, dissolved in 1 tablespoon water (or 2 teaspoons fresh lime juice)

1. Boil beef chuck in water 45 minutes. Let cool. Cut meat in 1-inch cubes.
2. In mixing bowl, make a paste from the marinade ingredients. Blend until smooth.
3. Mix the meat with the paste and let stand 2 hours.
4. Heat oil in skillet and fry meat over medium heat 5 minutes, or until it is brown and soft.
5. Drain on paper towels. Serve hot.

SERVES 4

Shin Ngoa Lap

LAOS

(Spicy Beef)

4 tablespoons glutinous rice

1 pound top round beef

2 teaspoons anchovy paste

2 teaspoon fish sauce

1 tablespoon dried *galangal* (soaked in water 1 hour, cut in strips)

1 tablespoon coriander leaves, chopped

1 tablespoon scallions, chopped

2 tablespoons lime juice

1 red chili, cored, seeded, sliced into rings

1. Pan toast glutinous rice in skillet. Transfer to a food processor and blend to make a powder.
2. Roast beef at 350°F for 30 minutes. Let cool. Shred into thin strips. Mix with powdered, browned glutinous rice. Set aside.
3. In a large pan over moderate heat, combine anchovy paste and fish sauce. Mix well. Add beef, *galangal*, coriander leaves, and chopped scallions. Stir well.
4. Arrange on platter and sprinkle with lime juice and chili before serving.
5. Serve hot.

SERVES 4

Gyuniku Teriyaki

JAPAN

(Broiled Marinated Beef)

- 2 pounds tenderloin or sirloin steak, ½- to 1-inch thick
- 2 teaspoons garlic, finely minced
- 2 tablespoons sugar
- ¼ cup sake or sherry
- ½ cup soy sauce
- 2 tablespoons Japanese horseradish powder (or mustard powder)
- 1 tablespoon hot water
- 1 teaspoon cornstarch

1. Combine minced garlic, sugar, sake, and soy sauce. Add beef and marinate overnight in refrigerator.
2. Dissolve horseradish powder in 1 tablespoon hot water (or more if needed) to make thick paste. Set aside.
3. Broil steak, browning on each side.
4. Add cornstarch to remaining marinade. Simmer in skillet to thicken, about 1 minute. Use as sauce.
5. When steak is cooked to desired doneness, slice in 1-inch strips. Serve hot on large platter, covered with sauce.
6. Serve horseradish separately.

SERVES 4

Sukiyaki

JAPAN

(Meat with Vegetables)

- ½ pound *shirataki* or vermicelli
- salted water
- 1 8-ounce can bamboo shoots
- 1 stalk celery
- 2 leeks
- 2 cups mushrooms
- 8 scallions
- 2 cups bean curd, cubed
- 1½ pounds beef tenderloin, thinly sliced
- 1 tablespoon beef fat
- 4 eggs, beaten

1. Cut vegetables into short lengths diagonally, about 1½ inches long.
2. Soak *shirataki* or vermicelli in salted water. Drain and set aside.

Warishita:

- 6 tablespoons soy sauce
- 6 tablespoons *mirin* or sherry
- 3 tablespoons sugar
- 1 cup water

1. Mix all the ingredients for the *warishita* in a saucepan. Bring to boil. Set aside.
2. Heat large pan. Rub bottom of pan with beef fat. Add bean curd, vermicelli, beef, vegetables, and *warishita* sauce. Simmer until cooked.
3. Serve hot. Meat and vegetables can be dipped into beaten eggs.

SERVES 4

Niku No Miso Yaki

JAPAN

(Meat with Miso)

- 2 pounds beef flank steak, cut in 1½-inch cubes
- 3 tablespoons soy sauce
- ¼ cup *akimiso* (Japanese red soybean paste)
- ½ cup scallions, minced
- 1 teaspoon fresh ginger root, grated
- 1½ tablespoons sugar
- 2 tablespoons vegetable oil
- ½ cup toasted sesame seeds

1. Place cubed flank steak with soy sauce, *akimiso*, scallions, ginger, and sugar in bowl. Marinate overnight in refrigerator.
2. Heat oil in a frying pan. Stir-fry meat and marinade mixture 5 minutes.
3. Serve hot. Garnish with toasted sesame seeds.

Serves 4

Poultry

Chicken was first linked to cuisine when the wild red jungle fowl *Gallus Gallus* was domesticated in Southwest Asia about 2000 B.C. At first considered a sacred bird used in prophecy and the divination of omens, and still the lord of the folk oracle, the chicken is now also one of the most popular ingredients of Asian cookery.

Of all the edible fowls known to man, it is perhaps the chicken that Asian cooks love most to prepare in a variety of ways. The white meat is particularly valued for its ability to absorb and blend with so many other flavors.

The preparation of chicken generally takes one of two forms: full-flavored and subtle-flavored. Either way, the cooking of chicken may be either complex or incredibly simple. The simplest manner is to skewer and roast the chicken with a marinade made from soy sauce or fish sauce and spiked with lemon and a bit of garlic. Whether broiled, roasted, steamed, baked, fried, boiled, fricasseed, stuffed, barbecued, or ground into pies or soups, chicken is superb, as it combines excellently with all other ingredients.

Because it is within the reach of any kitchen, and even raised in the backyard, the chicken is considered, as the Chinese poet Yuan Mei put it, one of the heroes of the Chinese table.

Other poultry known in Asian cuisines include the duck, which is a symbol of fidelity and happiness; the goose, a true gastronomic delight; the pigeon or squab, which stands for filial devotion and longevity; and the pheasant and quail, loved for their subtle flavors and exquisitely delicate taste. Turkey, a New World native, is generally served as a festive dish in the Philippines, the only Christianized Asian nation. It is presented at Christmas and Thanksgiving (which is celebrated in some parts of the Philippines), complete with stuffing in the American tradition.

Ayan Panggang Kecap

INDONESIA

(Barbecued Chicken in Soy Sauce)

1 chicken (2–3 pounds), cut in serving pieces

1 tablespoon vegetable oil

2 fresh chilies, finely minced

4 cloves garlic, finely minced

3 teaspoons fresh lemon juice

1 teaspoon sugar

¼ cup water

6 tablespoons sweet soy sauce

1 teaspoon ginger, sliced

1. Broil chicken pieces 5 minutes on each side.
2. Heat oil in large frying pan. Add chilies, garlic, lemon juice, sugar, water, soy sauce, and ginger. Simmer about 10 minutes (sauce will be fairly thick).
3. Transfer broiled chicken to frying pan with the thick sauce. Cook over medium heat 10 minutes, mixing the sauce with the chicken.
4. Return chicken to broiler. Broil another 5 minutes.
5. Serve hot.

SERVES 4

Petjel Ajam

INDONESIA

(Chicken in Coconut Milk)

1½ cups onion, finely minced

3 cloves garlic, finely minced

2 tablespoons vegetable oil

2 tablespoons coriander powder

4 cups coconut milk

3 tablespoons fresh ginger, diced

3 basil leaves

1 teaspoon ground chili

1 chicken (2–3 pounds), cooked, boned, and diced

1. Sauté onion and garlic in oil until onion becomes transparent.
2. Add coriander, coconut milk, ginger, basil, and chili. Simmer 10 minutes. Add diced chicken.
3. Continue simmering another 20 minutes, stirring frequently so mixture does not stick to pan.
4. Serve hot.

SERVES 4

Moan Chia Noeung Phset Kream

LAOS and CAMBODIA

(Stir-Fried Chicken with Mushrooms)

- 2 tablespoons vegetable oil
- 2 teaspoons garlic, finely minced
- 1 teaspoon fresh ginger root, finely minced
- 1 chicken (2–3 pounds), cut in serving pieces
- 8 dried Chinese mushrooms, soaked, drained, and cut in bite-size pieces
- 1 cup water
- 2 teaspoons sugar
- 2 tablespoons fish sauce
- 3 tablespoons fresh coriander leaves, chopped

1. Heat oil in large frying pan. Sauté garlic and ginger 1 minute. Add chicken. Stir well and cook 5 minutes.
2. Add mushrooms, water, sugar, and fish sauce. Simmer 20 minutes, or until chicken is cooked.
3. Serve hot. Garnish with fresh coriander leaves.

Serves 4

Mawk Kai

LAOS

(Chicken Steamed in Banana Leaf)

3 dried chili (soaked in water until soft)

2 cups shallots, chopped

4 stalks lemon grass, chopped (or 3 tablespoons lemon juice)

1 chicken (2–3 pounds), cut in serving pieces

½ tablespoon fish sauce

¼ teaspoon salt

1 cup scallions, finely minced

banana leaves or aluminum foil

1. Pound thoroughly chili, shallots, and lemon grass to a paste-like consistency.
2. Combine in mixing bowl the pounded ingredients and chicken.
3. Add fish sauce, salt, and ½ cup minced scallions.
4. Divide into 4 portions and wrap in banana leaves or aluminum foil.
5. Steam the 4 packages in a steamer 1 hour.
6. Open the packages and transfer the contents to a platter. Sprinkle remaining ½ cup minced scallions on top.

SERVES 4

Kai Pad Mak Phet Deng

LAOS

(Fried Chicken with Red Chili Peppers)

- 1 tablespoon vegetable oil
- 2 cups shallots, chopped
- 1 chicken (2–3 pounds), cut in serving pieces
- 2 teaspoons fish sauce
- 1 8-ounce can coconut milk
- 6 fresh red chili, seeded, cored, and soaked in water 15 minutes; then sliced julienne-style
- 12 scallions (whole with some of the green)
- ⅛ teaspoon black pepper, freshly ground
- ½ cup scallions, finely minced
- ½ cup fresh coriander leaves, chopped

1. Heat oil in large saucepan. Add chopped shallots and chicken pieces. Fry until chicken turns golden brown.
2. Add fish sauce and coconut milk. Simmer 15 minutes.
3. Add chili and whole scallions. Simmer 5 minutes longer.
4. Serve on a platter with black pepper, minced scallions, and coriander leaves as garnishing.

SERVES 4

Yakitori

JAPAN

(Broiled Chicken)

- skewers
- 1 chicken (2–3 pounds), boned and cut in 1½-inch squares
- 12 large scallions, cut in 2-inch pieces
- ¾ cup sake or sherry
- ¾ cup soy sauce
- 1 teaspoon fresh ginger root, grated
- ¼ cup sugar
- white pepper

1. On each skewer, thread 4 chicken pieces alternating with 3 pieces of scallion.
2. Combine sake, soy sauce, ginger, and sugar. Mix well. Baste chicken and scallions with mixture.
3. Broil over hot charcoal or in broiler, basting several times until meat is cooked.
4. Sprinkle with white pepper. Serve hot.

SERVES 6

Torimaki

JAPAN

(Chicken Omelette)

- 2 teaspoons *mirin* (or sherry)
- 1 teaspoon sugar
- ½ cup cooked chicken, finely chopped
- 3 teaspoons soy sauce
- 1 teaspoon fresh ginger root, finely grated
- 4 eggs
- 1 tablespoon water
- ¼ teaspoon salt
- 3 tablespoons vegetable oil

1. Thoroughly mix *mirin*, sugar, chicken, 2 teaspoons soy sauce, and grated ginger. Set aside.
2. Combine eggs, water, 1 teaspoon soy sauce, and salt. Mix well. Make an omelette with mixture using vegetable oil.
3. When omelette is nearly done, place filling in center, and fold over.
4. Serve immediately.

SERVES 4

Tatsuta Age

JAPAN

(Marinated Fried Chicken)

- 1 chicken (2–3 pounds), boned and cut in bite-size pieces
- 3 tablespoons sake
- 3 teaspoons sugar
- 6 tablespoons soy sauce
- 6 tablespoons cornstarch
- 1½ cups vegetable oil

1. Marinate chicken in sake, sugar, and soy sauce overnight.
2. Drain chicken and roll in cornstarch. Set aside for 10 minutes.
3. Heat oil in large saucepan, and fry chicken pieces until golden brown. Drain.
4. Serve hot.

SERVES 4

Arroz Caldo Con Pollo

THE PHILIPPINES

(Rice Chicken Soup)

3 tablespoons vegetable oil

2 tablespoons garlic, minced

¼ cup onion, chopped

8 ½-inch slices ginger

1 chicken (2–3½ pounds), cut in serving pieces

4 tablespoons fish sauce (or 2 tablespoons salt)

6 cups water

2 cups uncooked rice

¼ cup scallion, chopped

¼ teaspoon pepper, freshly ground

1. In a large covered stockpot, heat oil and sauté garlic, onion, and ginger until garlic is golden and onions transparent.
2. Add chicken and fish sauce (or salt.) Cover and simmer 5 minutes. (Chicken will produce its own juices.)
3. Add water and rice, stirring often to prevent sticking. Simmer 25 minutes over low heat, stirring often, until chicken and rice are tender.
4. Add chopped scallion and pepper before serving.

SERVES 6–8

Adobong Manok

THE PHILIPPINES

(Chicken Adobo)

1 chicken (3 pounds), cut in serving pieces

1½ cups soy sauce

¾ cup white vinegar

2 cloves garlic

2 bay leaves

½ teaspoon peppercorns

salt to taste

1. In a large stockpot, place chicken, soy sauce, vinegar, garlic, bay leaves, and peppercorns. Simmer 1 hour.
2. Remove chicken and broil in a separate pan until golden. Set aside.
3. Continue boiling sauce in stockpot until reduced by half. Add salt to taste.
4. Place chicken in serving dish and cover with sauce.
5. Serve hot.

SERVES 6

Apritadang Manok

THE PHILIPPINES

(Chicken Apritada-Style)

- 1 chicken (2–3 pounds), cut in serving pieces
- 1 clove garlic, crushed
- ¼ cup chopped onion
- 1 6-ounce can tomato sauce
- 1 bay leaf
- 1 tablespoon peppercorns
- 2 teaspoons salt
- 1 teaspoon pepper
- ¼ cup water
- 2 medium size potatoes, cubed
- 1 4-ounce can pimentos

1. In saucepan, combine chicken pieces, garlic, onion, tomato sauce, bay leaf, peppercorns, salt, pepper, and water. Simmer 15 minutes.
2. Add cubed potatoes and pimentos. Simmer until potatoes are tender.
3. Serve hot.

SERVES 4

Pocherong Manok

THE PHILIPPINES

(Chicken Pochero-Style)

- 1 chicken (2½–3 pounds)
- water
- 1 *chorizo de Bilbao* (or pepperoni)
- 10 peppercorns
- salt to taste
- 2 plantain bananas, whole
- 2 small potatoes, peeled and quartered
- ½ small green cabbage, quartered
- ½ small head *bok choy*, cut in 2-inch slices
- 1 clove garlic, crushed
- 1 small onion, diced
- 1 8-ounce can tomato sauce
- 2 tablespoons vegetable oil
- ½ cup water
- 1 8-ounce can chick peas, drained

1. Place chicken in stewpot with enough water to cover. Add sausage, peppercorns, and salt. Cook until chicken is tender. Drain and reserve the stock and set other ingredients aside.
2. Boil plantains separately (10 minutes if green, 5 minutes if ripe). Peel after cooking and set aside.
3. Using drained chicken stock, boil potatoes until done. Add cabbage and bok choy and set aside.
4. Sauté the garlic, onion, tomato sauce, chicken, and sausage in 2 tablespoons of oil, until chicken begins to brown. Add ½ cup of water and the chick peas, and continue to cook about 10 minutes.
5. Transfer chicken and sausage mixture to a serving platter. Remove potatoes, bok choy, and cabbage from stock and serve alongside.

SERVES 4–6

Sinigang Na Manok

THE PHILIPPINES

(Boiled Chicken with Vegetables)

- 1 chicken (2 pounds), cut in serving pieces
- ½ cup tomatoes, sliced
- ¼ cup onion, sliced
- juice of 1 lemon
- water for boiling
- 1 cup green beans, cut in 2-inch pieces
- 1 cup small radishes, quartered
- 1 small bunch of green leafy vegetable (broccoli, spinach, rabe or collard greens)
- 1 tablespoon salt (or fish sauce)

1. Boil chicken, tomatoes, onion, and lemon juice in enough water to cover chicken.
2. Cook until chicken is almost tender.
3. Add rest of ingredients. Continue cooking until chicken is fully tender and vegetables are crisp-tender.
4. Serve hot.

SERVES 4

Dak Jim

KOREA

(Chicken Stew)

1 chicken (2–3 pounds), cut in serving pieces

½ teaspoon salt

½ cup scallions, finely chopped

¾ cup soy sauce

2 tablespoons sesame oil

½ teaspoon chili powder

1½ tablespoons garlic, minced

1. In a large covered saucepan, combine chicken and all other ingredients. Marinate for 3 hours in refrigerator.
2. Cover saucepan and cook over low heat 45 minutes to 1 hour, or until chicken is tender.
3. Serve hot.

Serves 2

Dak Busut Jim

KOREA

(Braised Mushroom and Chicken)

- 1 tablespoon garlic, finely minced
- 1 tablespoon sesame oil
- 4 tablespoons soy sauce
- ½ teaspoon chili powder
- ½ teaspoon ground black pepper
- 1 chicken (2–3 pounds), cut in serving pieces
- 3 tablespoons vegetable oil
- 12 dried Chinese mushrooms, soaked in hot water and cut in thin strips (discard stems)
- 1 cup mushroom water
- 1½ cups onion, chopped
- ½ cup scallions, minced
- 2 winter bamboo shoots (canned), thinly sliced
- 3 tablespoons sesame seeds, toasted and crushed

1. In large mixing bowl, combine garlic, sesame oil, soy sauce, chili powder, pepper, and chicken. Marinate 2 hours.
2. Remove chicken from marinade. Heat oil in a large frying pan and stir-fry chicken until brown.
3. Add mushrooms and 1 cup mushroom water.
4. Add marinade, cover, and simmer 20 minutes, (or until chicken is tender).
5. Add onion, scallions, and bamboo shoots. Simmer 5 minutes longer.
6. Serve hot, garnished with sesame seeds.

SERVES 4

Gulay Ayam Rebong (I)

MALAYSIA

(Chicken and Asparagus or Bamboo Shoots)

- 2 chicken breasts, sliced ½-inch thick
- 2 teaspoons ginger juice
- ⅛ teaspoon salt
- ⅛ teaspoon pepper
- 2 tablespoons soy sauce
- 4 tablespoons vegetable oil
- 2 teaspoons garlic, finely minced
- 2 tablespoons all-purpose flour
- ½ cup heavy cream
- 1 8-ounce can asparagus spears or bamboo shoots (reserve liquid)
- ⅛ teaspoon salt
- ⅛ teaspoon pepper

1. Marinate chicken breast slices with ginger juice, salt, pepper, and soy sauce 1 hour.
2. Stir-fry chicken pieces in 3 tablespoons vegetable oil. Set aside.
3. Place 1 tablespoon oil in large saucepan, and sauté garlic until golden. Add flour and fry 2 minutes (do not let flour burn).
4. Add heavy cream and 1 cup asparagus or bamboo water. Stir well until mixture becomes smooth.
5. Drop chicken slices and asparagus or bamboo shoots into mixture. Simmer 5 minutes. Serve hot.

SERVES 4

Gulay Ayam Rebong (II)

MALAYSIA

(Chicken and Bamboo Shoot Curry)

- 3 tablespoons vegetable oil
- 2 cups onion, finely minced
- 1½ teaspoons dried shrimp paste
- 1 teaspoon *laos* powder
- 1 tablespoon ground coriander
- 1 teaspoon chili powder
- 2 teaspoons salt
- 1 chicken (2½–3 pounds), cut in serving pieces
- 3 cups coconut milk
- 1 8-ounce can bamboo shoots, drained and sliced in ⅛-inch thick pieces

1. Heat oil in large saucepan and sauté onion until transparent.
2. Add shrimp paste, *laos* powder, coriander, chili powder, and salt. Stir constantly until mixture is brown.
3. Add stewing fowl and coconut milk. Simmer over moderate heat, stirring frequently, 45 minutes, or until chicken is tender.
4. Add bamboo shoots and simmer 5 minutes more.
5. Serve hot.

SERVES 6

Rendang Ayam

MALAYSIA

(Chicken in Coconut Milk)

2 tablespoons garlic, finely minced

2 cups onions, chopped

3 teaspoons fresh ginger root, finely minced

3 fresh red chilies

½ cup fresh lemon grass, sliced

2 cups coconut milk

1 teaspoon ground coriander

1 teaspoon *laos* powder

1 teaspoon turmeric, ground

5 curry leaves

1 teaspoon salt

½ teaspoon ground black pepper

1 stewing fowl (4–5 pounds), cut in serving pieces

1. In food processor, puree garlic, onions, ginger, chili, lemon grass, and coconut milk.
2. Transfer to a large saucepan. Add coriander, *laos* powder, turmeric, curry leaves, salt, and pepper. Bring to a slow boil.
3. Add chicken. Simmer until chicken is tender.
4. Serve hot, with rice as side dish.

SERVES 6

Yu Ling Chi

CHINA

(Deep Fried Chicken)

- 1 chicken (2–3 pounds)
- ¼ teaspoon pepper
- ¼ teaspoon salt
- 4 tablespoons soy sauce
- 3 tablespoons dry sherry
- 3 cups vegetable oil

Sauce:

- 1 tablespoon fresh parsley, finely minced
- 1 tablespoon onion, finely minced
- 1 teaspoon fresh ginger root, finely minced
- 3 tablespoons soy sauce
- 1 tablespoon Chinese wine
- 1 tablespoon sugar
- 1 tablespoon vinegar

Garnish:

- 1 16-ounce can sliced pineapple, drained

1. Sprinkle chicken with pepper and salt. Marinate in soy sauce and sherry for 2 hours.
2. Heat oil in deep frying pan and fry chicken until brown. Drain. Cut chicken in serving pieces.
3. Combine all sauce ingredients in bowl. Mix well.
4. Place chicken in deep platter. Pour sauce over chicken.
5. Garnish with pineapple slices.

SERVES 4

See Yo Gai

CHINA

(Red-Cooked Chicken)

- 2 cups dark soy sauce
- 2 cups water
- ½ cup dry sherry
- 3 tablespoons fresh ginger root, minced
- 2 teaspoons garlic, minced
- 2 tablespoons sugar
- ½ teaspoon star anise
- 3 teaspoons sesame oil
- 1 roasting chicken (2½–3½ pounds)

1. Combine all ingredients except chicken. Mix well.
2. Place chicken breast down in large saucepan. Pour mixture over chicken to cover.
3. Bring chicken and mixture to a boil. Lower heat and simmer, uncovered, 30 minutes. Turn chicken and continue simmering 20 minutes longer.
4. Cover pan and remove from heat. Let stand covered until cool.
5. Cut chicken into serving pieces, place on a platter, and brush with sesame oil.
6. Serve immediately with remaining sauce as a dip.

SERVES 6

Shiu Ng Heung Gai

CHINA

(Oven-Roasted Spiced Chicken)

- 1 chicken (2–3 pounds), cut in serving pieces
- 1 tablespoon dry sherry
- ½ cup soy sauce
- ¼ cup peanut oil
- ½ teaspoon salt
- 2 teaspoons garlic, finely minced
- ½ teaspoon fresh ginger root, finely grated
- 2 teaspoons Five Spice Powder

1. Combine all ingredients in mixing bowl. Mix well. Marinate chicken pieces in refrigerator overnight.
2. Remove chicken from marinade and place in roasting pan. Roast in a 350°F oven until brown and crisp (about 1 hour). Baste occasionally with marinade.
3. Serve hot.

SERVES 6

Yahng Gai

THAILAND

(Chicken Barbecue)

1 chicken (2–3 pounds), quartered

Marinade:

4 teaspoons garlic, finely minced

1 teaspoon coriander, ground

1 cup coconut milk

½ teaspoon turmeric, ground

½ teaspoon salt

1 teaspoon black pepper, freshly ground

1. In mixing bowl, combine all marinade ingredients. Mix thoroughly.
2. Marinate chicken in refrigerator overnight.
3. Broil chicken in oven or barbecue over hot coals. Baste occasionally with marinade.
4. Serve hot.

SERVES 4

Gai Paht King

THAILAND

(Chicken with Ginger)

2 tablespoons vegetable oil

2 teaspoons garlic, finely minced

3 fresh green chili peppers, thinly shredded

1 chicken (2–3 pounds), boned, skinned, and coarsely shredded

4 ounces fresh ginger root, shredded, soaked in water 15 minutes, and drained

3 tablespoons small wood fungus, soaked in water 15 minutes, and drained

2 tablespoons fish sauce

3 tablespoons water

2 tablespoons soy sauce

1. Heat oil in large frying pan. Add garlic and chili pepper. Stir-fry until garlic turns golden.
2. Add chicken, ginger root, and wood fungus. Stir-fry 5 minutes.
3. Add fish sauce, water, and soy sauce. Stir-fry 3 minutes longer.
4. Serve hot.

Serves 4

Vit Nuong

VIETNAM

(Roast Duck)

5 garlic cloves, finely minced

1½ teaspoon sugar

1½ tablespoon fresh ginger root, finely chopped or grated

¾ cup soy sauce

1 duck (3½–4 pounds)

1. Combine garlic, sugar, ginger, and soy sauce. Mix well.
2. Rub mixture on duck. Marinate in refrigerator overnight.
3. Heat oven to 350°F. Place duck on a rack in a roasting pan. Roast 2 hours, or until done. Brush occasionally with marinade.
4. Serve hot.

SERVES 4–6

Ga Tim

VIETNAM

(Stuffed Chicken)

1 chicken (2–3 pounds)

water for boiling

1 quart chicken stock

2 tablespoons fish sauce

Stuffing:

½ cup roasted almonds, slivered

12 dried mushrooms, soaked in warm water till soft, then cut julienne style

½ pound ground pork

6 shallots, finely minced

½ teaspoon black pepper, finely ground

3 tablespoons fish sauce

1. Mix stuffing ingredients very well. Stuff chicken with mixture.
2. In deep cooking pot, steam chicken over boiling water 1 hour.
3. Remove chicken from steamer. In another pot, combine chicken stock and fish sauce and add cooked chicken. Bring to boil, reduce heat, and continue to simmer for 15 minutes.

3\. Serve on a large platter.

SERVES 4

Ga Hap Ca

VIETNAM

(Stir-Fried Chicken and Tomatoes)

1 chicken (2–3 pounds), cut in serving pieces

3 tablespoons shallots, finely minced

1 teaspoon salt

1 teaspoon pepper

4 tablespoons vegetable oil

3 cloves garlic, finely minced

2 cups tomatoes, minced

2 tablespoons tomato paste

1½ tablespoons fish sauce

1. Marinate chicken with 1 tablespoon shallots, salt, and pepper 2 hours.
2. Heat oil in a large frying pan and brown chicken.
3. Add garlic, tomatoes, 2 tablespoons shallots, tomato paste, and fish sauce. Simmer 20 minutes.
4. Serve hot.

SERVES 4

Hmo Kyaw Kyet

BURMA

(Burmese Roast Chicken)

- 1 chicken (2–3 pounds), cut in serving pieces
- 2 tablespoons thick soy sauce
- ½ teaspoon cayenne pepper
- ¾ teaspoon ground black pepper
- ⅓ cup vegetable oil
- 2 inches ginger root, cut julienne-style
- 1½ cups water
- 2 medium onions, sliced
- 1 head garlic, crushed
- ½ cup dried mushrooms, soaked in water
- salt and pepper to taste

1. Marinate chicken in mixture of soy sauce, cayenne pepper, and black pepper.
2. Heat vegetable oil in skillet and fry ginger until brown (about 6 minutes). Remove ginger.
3. Remove chicken from marinade, pat dry, and fry in skillet until brown.
4. Add 1 cup water, the marinade, and ½ the fried ginger. Cover, and simmer until chicken is tender.
5. Add onions, garlic, mushrooms, and ½ cup water. Continue simmering until partly dry. Add salt and pepper to taste.
6. Transfer chicken to platter, pour remaining sauce and the rest of the fried ginger over chicken.

SERVES 4

Desserts

Dessert cookery in Asia is not as extensive as that of America or Europe. Asians generally are not fond of desserts *per se*, traditionally preferring to serve sweet dishes during the course of a meal to further stimulate the tastebuds or to remove some of the lingering richness of main courses. More often, sweets are taken during the day as snacks. However, in modern times, the Western custom of serving a sweet dish at the end of a meal is becoming more prevalent.

Many of the Asian sweets feature rice cooked in coconut milk, garnished with fresh fruits. Preserved fruits are also popular, and baked pastries are becoming more widely served. Native fruits of the area, such as mangoes, which come in many varieties and are so popular that they are called the "apples of the tropics," and bananas, which also come in many varieties, sizes, and degrees of sweetness, are the bases for such dishes as steamed rice cakes, baked fruit or butter cakes, ice cream, sherbets, fritters, and glazed fruits. In Thailand, home of many fruits of delectable flavor, fresh fruits are carved by skilled artists into shapes of flowers, other fruits, or birds.

In whatever manner Asian ingredients are used to make sweet dishes, one still finds that special gourmet touch and the endless creativity which is the heart of all Asian cuisines.

Kuay Namuan

CAMBODIA

(Wrapped Bananas)

- 3 cups glutinous rice
- water
- 1 8-ounce can coconut milk
- ¼ teaspoon salt
- 20 6-inch squares aluminum foil (or 20 banana leaves)
- 8 ripe bananas, each peeled and sliced lengthwise and crosswise to produce 4 finger-size pieces
- 3 tablespoons sesame seeds
- 2 cups coconut, grated

1. Soak glutinous rice in water overnight. Drain and transfer to a mixing bowl.
2. Add coconut milk and salt.
3. On each piece of foil or banana leaf, place 2 teaspoons rice and coconut milk mixture. Top with banana finger and cover with another 2 teaspoons rice and coconut milk mixture.
4. Fold each into an oblong package and steam on rack in steamer 1 hour.
5. Toast sesame seeds in skillet 3 minutes. Cool and crush lightly.
6. Unwrap each package and sprinkle with sesame seeds and grated coconut. Serve hot.

SERVES 8

Che Khoai Lang

VIETNAM

(Sweet-Potato Pudding)

- 4 medium sweet potatoes, peeled and cut in ½-inch cubes
- 8 cups water
- 4 tablespoons sugar
- 1 tablespoon vanilla extract

1. In saucepan, cook sweet potatoes in water until tender (about 40 minutes).
2. Add sugar and vanilla. Simmer another 10 minutes.
3. Serve hot or cold.

SERVES 4–6

Che Bap

VIETNAM

(Sweet Corn Pudding)

- 4 ears corn (or 1 8-ounce can sweet corn)
- 1 quart water
- 6 tablespoons sugar

1. Separate corn kernels from cobs. Puree corn kernels in food processor.
2. Heat corn and water in a saucepan over medium heat. Add sugar and continue to cook, stirring, for 20 minutes.
3. Serve hot or cold.

SERVES 4

Leche Flan

THE PHILIPPINES

(Crème Caramel)

Caramel:

1 cup sugar

¼ cup water

1. Bring sugar and water to a boil. Stir continuously over medium heat until sugar melts and begins to turn brown.
2. Pour caramelized syrup into flan mold or custard cups, tilting mold to make sure all surfaces are covered.

Custard:

12 egg yolks

2 13-ounce cans evaporated milk

1 14-ounce can sweetened condensed milk

1 teaspoon vanilla

1 can *macapuno* (optional)

1. In large bowl, combine custard ingredients. Stir lightly when mixing to prevent bubbles or foam from forming.
2. Strain slowly while pouring into caramel-lined flan mold.
3. Preheat oven 325°F. Cover mold with aluminum foil. Place mold in larger tray filled with water.
4. Bake in oven 1 hour, or until mixture is firm.
5. Cool before unmolding on to platter. If desired, top with *macapuno*.

SERVES 10

Polvoron

THE PHILIPPINES

(Powdered Milk Candy)

3 cups flour, sifted

1 cup powdered milk, sifted

¾ cup sugar, sifted

½ pound butter, melted

1 teaspoon lemon or vanilla extract

1. Toast flour in heavy skillet or saucepan over moderate heat until light brown, stirring constantly. Remove from heat and cool.
2. Add powdered milk, sugar, melted butter, and lemon or vanilla extract.
3. Form little cakes, about 1½ inches in diameter and about ¼-inch high.
4. Wrap individually in waxed paper or plastic wrap.

YIELD: ABOUT 20 CANDIES

Espasol

THE PHILIPPINES

(Sweet Rice Flour Cakes)

4 cups sweet rice flour

1½ cups sugar

2 cans coconut milk

½ teaspoon salt

1. Toast sweet rice flour on greased cookie sheet. Set aside 1 cup.
2. Bring sugar, coconut milk, and salt to a boil.
3. Add 3 cups toasted sweet rice flour. Mix well and simmer until thick, stirring constantly.
4. Remove from heat and transfer to board that has been well sprinkled with ½ cup reserved sweet rice flour.
5. With a rolling pin, flatten to about ¼-inch thick and cut into diamonds.
6. Roll in remaining rice flour.

YIELD: 15 TO 20 CAKES

Brazo de Mercedes

THE PHILIPPINES

(Creme-filled Log Cake)

Filling:

- 5 cups milk
- 1 cup sugar
- 2 tablespoons unsalted butter
- 1 tablespoon vanilla extract
- 8 egg yolks
- ¼ cup toasted cashew nuts, finely ground

1. In saucepan, simmer milk over low heat until reduced to 2 cups.
2. Add sugar, butter, and vanilla extract, stirring constantly. Remove from heat.
3. Beat egg yolks in mixing bowl. Gradually add milk mixture by spoonfuls, beating constantly to avoid curdling. Return to saucepan.
4. Add cashew nuts and continue cooking entire mixture over low heat, stirring constantly, until mixture has consistency of a paste. Set aside.

Meringue:

- 10 egg whites
- 1 cup sugar
- 1 teaspoon vanilla extract

1. Preheat oven to 400°F.

4. Beat egg whites until stiff. Gradually add sugar, beating continuously. Stir in vanilla.

3. Line large cookie sheet with parchment paper greased with butter and spread meringue on top. Bake until brown.

4. Spread filling evenly on top of meringue and roll into log shape.

5. Brush with butter. Return to oven briefly. Remove when lightly browned.

SERVES 6–8

Ginataang Mongo

THE PHILIPPINES

(Bean Pudding)

2 cups mung beans

2 cups glutinous sweet rice

1 cup coconut milk

1 cup coconut cream

5 tablespoons sugar

1. Brown mung beans in oil in skillet until crisp.
2. Crush beans with rolling pin.
3. Mix beans and rice.
4. In a medium pot, simmer the mixture in coconut milk over moderate heat 30 minutes. Remove from heat.
5. Add coconut cream and sugar.

SERVES 8

Suspiros de Casuy

THE PHILIPPINES

(Candied Cashew Nuts)

- 2 cups sugar
- 1 cup water
- 2 tablespoons corn syrup
- 1 cup cashew nuts (or almonds, hazelnuts, walnuts)

1. In a saucepan, caramelize sugar by boiling sugar and water together.
2. Add corn syrup when mixture becomes sticky.
3. Arrange nuts on cookie sheet, and pour syrup over nuts.
4. With fork, gradually pull individual nuts apart so as to form threads.
5. Pack in airtight bottles, jars, or cans lined with waxed paper or plastic wrap.

YIELD: 1 CUP

Ji-Dahn Goh

CHINA

(Sweet Custard)

- 6 tablespoons sugar
- 1½ cups warm water
- 3 teaspoons vanilla extract
- 4 eggs
- 5 cups cold water
- 1 cup sugar

1. Dissolve 6 tablespoons sugar, warm water, and 2 teaspoons vanilla extract in mixing bowl.
2. Beat eggs lightly and pour into mixing bowl with sugar, water, and vanilla.
3. Strain mixture and place strained liquid in large soup bowl.
4. Place bowl in steamer and steam over moderate heat 20 minutes, or until firm.
5. In a pan, combine cold water, sugar, and 1 teaspoon vanilla extract. Boil for 10 minutes.
6. Cut egg custard in ½-inch cubes, place in a bowl, and pour over it boiled water, sugar, and vanilla mixture.

SERVES 10

Kow Hwa Sun

CHINA

(Nutty-Milk Dessert)

- 1 cup shelled, unsalted, roasted peanuts (or cashew nuts)
- oil for frying
- ½ cup sesame seeds
- 6 cups water
- ¾ cup sugar
- 3 tablespoons cornstarch, mixed with 3 tablespoons water
- ¾ cup evaporated milk

1. Remove skin from peanuts.
2. In frying pan, stir-fry sesame seeds in oil until golden brown.
3. Place peanuts, sesame seeds, and 1 cup water in food processor and blend until smooth.
4. Place mixture into pan. Add 5 cups water and sugar. Bring to boil, reduce heat, and add cornstarch to thicken.
5. Add evaporated milk and mix well.
6. Serve warm.

SERVES 6

Kow Hwa Sun Tong

CHINA

(Sweet Peanut Soup)

⅔ cup unsalted roasted peanuts, shelled

10 cups water

1 cup sugar

1. In large saucepan, place peanuts with water to cover. Boil 5 minutes. Drain and let cool. Remove skins from peanuts.
2. Place skinned nuts in covered pan and simmer with water over moderate heat about an hour and a quarter, or until peanuts are very tender.
3. Add sugar, and more water if necessary, and bring to a boil until sugar dissolves.
4. Serve hot or cold.

SERVES 10

Kluay Buat Chee

THAILAND

(Bananas in Coconut Milk)

1 8-ounce can coconut milk

6 ripe bananas, peeled and quartered

2 tablespoons sugar

¼ teaspoon salt

3 tablespoons roasted mung beans, crushed

1. In saucepan, bring coconut milk, bananas, sugar, and salt to boil. Simmer over moderate heat 5 minutes.
2. Transfer to a serving dish and sprinkle with crushed roasted mung beans.

SERVES 4

Agar-Agar

MALAYSIA

(Agar-Agar Jelly)

- 6 cups water
- 4 teaspoons agar-agar powder (sold in Oriental stores)
- 1 cup sugar
- 1½ teaspoons vanilla extract
- 6 drops almond extract

1. Boil agar-agar powder in water until it dissolves. Add sugar and stir until sugar dissolves.
2. Add vanilla and almond extracts.
3. Pour into a glass bowl and refrigerate.
4. Serve chilled.

Serves 4

Sri Kaya

MALAYSIA

(Coconut Custard)

1 cup date palm sugar

1 cup water

10 eggs, lightly beaten

1 cup coconut milk

1. In a saucepan, boil date palm sugar with water. Stir until sugar is dissolved. Set aside.
2. Place beaten eggs in ovenproof bowl and add coconut milk and palm sugar syrup. Stir well and blend.
3. Place bowl in a large pan with a tightly fitting lid. Steam over rapidly boiling water 45 minutes.
4. Serve hot or cold.

SERVES 6

Kuay Namuan

LAOS

(Bananas Cooked in Coconut Milk)

1 8-ounce can coconut milk

3 tablespoons sugar

8 large ripe bananas, peeled, each cut in 3 pieces

1. Simmer coconut milk and sugar in saucepan over moderate heat until thick (about 20 minutes).
2. Add bananas and cook until they are soft (about 10 minutes).
3. Serve warm.

SERVES 6

Ping Manton

LAOS

(Grilled Cassava)

2 pounds young cassava roots (or sweet potatoes), peeled

½ cup sugar

1 8-ounce can coconut milk

1. Grill or broil cassava roots until soft. Remove from heat and flatten.
2. Combine sugar and coconut milk. Mix well.
3. Dip flattened pieces of cassava in the mixture and grill 5 minutes under low fire.
4. Serve hot.

SERVES 6

Khao Tom Mak Kuay

LAOS

(Steamed Rice and Banana Puddings)

½ pound glutinous rice, soaked in water 5 hours

1 8-ounce can coconut milk

¼ pound sugar

¼ teaspoon salt

12 banana leaves (or aluminum foil pieces, 8 inches square)

3 bananas, cut in half lengthwise, then again crosswise

1. In large saucepan, bring rice and coconut milk to boil. Stir well and simmer the mixture 20 minutes.
2. Add sugar and salt and mix well. Set aside.
3. On banana leaves or aluminum foil, drop 2 tablespoons of rice and coconut mixture and put a banana slice on top. Wrap to make package. Repeat until all bananas and mixture have been used.
4. Steam packages 30 minutes and serve.

SERVES 12

Yokan

JAPAN

(Red Bean Cake)

2 cups water

2 pieces agar-agar square (about ¼ ounce)

2 cups sugar

2 cups red bean paste, strained

½ teaspoon salt

1. Boil agar-agar in water. Add sugar and continue boiling until sugar is dissolved.
2. Strain into another saucepan. Add red bean paste and salt. Cook over moderate heat, stirring continually, until mixture is thick and has a starch-like consistency.
3. Pour into an 8- or 9-inch square pan. When cooled, cut into 1½-inch squares.

SERVES 8

Mizu-Yokan

JAPAN

(Sweetened Red Bean Paste)

2 cups *azuki* (red beans)
water for soaking
2 teaspoons salt
2 cups sugar

1. Soak beans 10–12 hours in water. Change water once or twice.
2. Boil beans in large pot until shells are broken and beans are soft.
3. Drain beans and place in a food processor. Process gently to a paste-like consistency.
4. Place bean paste in a coarse muslin bag and gently squeeze out as much water as possible.
5. Transfer paste to a saucepan. Cook over low fire. Gradually add salt and sugar, stirring until paste is thick and sugar dissolved.
6. Use as ingredient for various sweets.

Glossary

Achuete (also *achiote*)—Food coloring used in the Philippines to give a reddish color, made from *anatto* seeds (see below). Available in bottles.
Agar-agar—A gelatinous product made from seaweed, used in jellied and preserved foods; available in powder form or as jelly-like blocks.
Akimiso—Japanese red soybean paste.
Anatto water—Preparation made from anatto seeds, used in the Philippines for food coloring. To prepare in any quantity, place 1 part anatto seeds in 4 parts water and crush seeds between fingers to release red color. Let stand 30 minutes, then strain water and discard seeds.
Azuki—Japanese red beans.

Bagoong—A salty, fermented sauce or paste made from small shrimps or fish, used in the Philippines as an accompaniment to main dishes (see *shrimp paste*).
Blacan—The Malaysian version of shrimp paste (see *shrimp paste*).
Bok choy—Chinese cabbage; this member of the mustard family has long, pale leaves growing in loose, cylindrical heads, and tastes somewhat like cabbage. It is readily available in vegetable stores and in some supermarkets.
Buah keras—Candlenuts, the waxy fruit of the Pacific tree, used primarily for oil (in cooking) or to make candles.

Chorizo de Bilbao—A Spanish sausage used in the Philippines for flavoring dishes; pepperoni sausage makes a reasonably close substitute.
Curry leaves—Leaves resembling bay laurel, used in Malaysian and Indonesian curries. Available dried in Indian and Southeast Asian food shops.

Daikon—A white Japanese radish.
Dashi—A Japanese sauce ingredient prepared by boiling together for 15 minutes the following ingredients: 5 cups water, 1 cup flaked ***katsuobushi*** (dried bonito fillet), 1 square inch dried ***konbu*** (seaweed or kelp), 1 teaspoon soy sauce, and 1 teaspoon salt. Makes 5 cups.
Date palm sugar—Coarse, sticky brown sugar made from palm sap, this is less sweet than ordinary cane sugar. Available canned or in cakes. A combination of half refined or raw brown sugar and half molasses may be substituted for an equal amount of palm sugar.

Fish sauce—A popular ingredient throughout Southeast Asia, where it is used in a number of different types of recipes, this is a thin, very salty liquid extract of salted and/or fermented seafood (usually fish). Known as ***patis*** in the Philippines, ***nuoc mam*** in Vietnam, ***nam pla*** in Thailand, and ***ngan pya ye*** in Burma, all are generally interchangeable. If you choose not to use fish sauce in any recipe that calls for it, additional salt (to taste) must be added.
Five Spice Powder—A combination of Chinese spices including star anise, fennel, Szechuan peppercorns, clove, and cinnamon. The preparation is available ready-mixed.

Galangal (also ***galingale***)—The root of a ginger-like plant, having a gingery-peppery taste. The dried root is available whole or ground. Also called *Laos.*

Hoi sin sauce—A Chinese prepared sauce with a wheat or soybean base, usually containing vinegar, chilies, garlic, and sesame. It generally has a tart-sweet, fruity flavor and the consistency of fruit preserves.

Krung gaeng pad—Thai red curry paste, available in jars and packets.
Katsuobushi—Dried bonito fillet, used as a base for Japanese broths and sauces.
Konbu—Dried seaweed or kelp, used in Japanese cooking.
Ketjap—In Malaysia and Indonesia, a sauce based on soy or fish.
Kway teow—Malaysian rice noodles.

Lemon grass—A plant generally resembling a scallion, with long leaves and a large bulb, prized for its lemony, aromatic flavor. If fresh lemon grass is unobtainable, powdered lemon grass or dried stems (available from specialty stores) may be substituted.
Laos powder—A powder made from dried ***galangal*** (see above).

Macapuno—Preserved strips of white coconut meat in a sweetened syrup, popular in the Philippines.

Maggi sauce—A salty, liquid seasoning used in Filipino cooking. Maggi is a brand name.
Meehon—Malaysian fine rice vermicelli.
Miki—Filipino rice noodles.
Mirin—A sweetened and lightly syrupy Japanese cooking wine. Sweet sherry is an acceptable substitute.
Miso—Japanese prepared sauce made from fermented, salted, soft black soybeans.
Misua—Filipino threadlike wheat noodles, or vermicelli.
Mung beans—Small, green beans from which bean sprouts are produced.

Nam pla—Thai version of fish sauce (see ***fish sauce***).
Ngan pya ye—The Burmese version of fish sauce (see ***fish sauce***).
Ngapi—Burmese shrimp paste (see ***shrimp paste***).
Nori—Dried laver seaweed. Available in thin, greenish-black sheets resembling carbon paper, it becomes crisper and takes on a purplish color when warmed.
Nuoc mam—Vietnamese fish sauce (see ***fish sauce***).

Patis—Filipino fish sauce (see ***fish sauce***).

Sake—Japanese rice wine.
Sambal badjak—A hot paste used in Indonesia as a condiment. To prepare, combine ½ cup red chili soaked in ½ cup water for ½ hour, 2 cloves finely minced garlic, 2 tablespoons finely minced onions, 1 teaspoon shrimp paste, 1 teaspoon salt, 1 teaspoon sugar, and 1 teaspoon tamarind paste dissolved in 1 tablespoon water. Blend all the ingredients to a paste-like consistency in a food processor. In a saucepan, heat 2 tablespoons vegetable oil, add the mixture, and cook until the liquid has evaporated, about 15 mintues.
Shirataki—A long, vermicelli-like thread noodle, used in Japanese cooking.
Shrimp paste—A condiment used throughout Southeast Asia, this is a thick, salty paste of fermented shrimp, often sold in small rolls. Known as ***bagoong*** in the Philippines, ***blacan*** in Malaysia, ***trassi*** in Indonesia, and ***ngapi*** in Burma.
Sotanghon—Filipino bean noodles.

Tamarind paste—A paste made from the dried pulp of the tamarind, a tart, brown fruit.
Trassi—Indonesian shrimp paste (see ***shrimp paste***).

Udon—Thick noodles made from wheat flour. No. 2 spaghetti is an acceptable substitute.

Index